Manipulation

Highly Effective Persuasion and Manipulation Techniques People of Power Use for Deception and Influence, Including 7 Laws of Human Behavior, NLP Tips, and Strategies of Dark Psychology

Contents

Introduction

Manipulation is an incredible art form that allows people to get what they want when they want it effortlessly. Because it requires a basic understanding of human psychology and the skills to manipulate human psychology, many people wrongfully believe that manipulation is difficult and requires years of study and practice. The reality is quite the opposite.

If you want it to be, manipulation can be an easy and effective strategy to help you get anything you want in life. Whether you want to win over more clients, earn a better salary at work, borrow money, crash on someone's couch for a night, negotiate better deals, or anything else, manipulation is a great way to make that happen.

Forget the outdated belief that manipulation is cruel or conning. The truth is: manipulation is a powerful negotiating tool that allows you to stay in the driver's seat and command anything you want in life. The days of using guilt and fear are long gone, as manipulation has officially become a powerful tool to use in business and life in general. If you want to be a true master manipulator, it is extremely simple and causes no feeling of guilt or shame in you or your target. Instead, it is a mere tool that you use to get what you want when you want it.

This book will help you learn how you can be a master of manipulation and get anything you want. You will read about the three steps of manipulation, including analysis, manipulation, and persuasion. You will also be given very clear facts about why each step is necessary, how it works, and what is required to make it work. Each technique you are given will be clearly explained, and in some, you are also given real-life examples to ensure that you completely understand why and how they work. This will allow you to see them in action so that you can become inspired to use them in your own daily life.

If you want to command your life, get what you want, and get to where you want to go, manipulation is a necessary strategy to master. However, there is no need to master all the techniques completely. To get the most out of your practice, you simply need the ones that have already been outlined in this easy guide book. Once you master these and begin putting them into practice, you will be able to manipulate people like a pro. The best part is: no one will even know that you are doing it. It will seem as though your target is the one making all the decisions, even though you're the one secretly pulling the puppet strings to make it happen. If you are ready to learn how to, let's begin!

Chapter 1: What Is Manipulation?

Manipulation is using people's emotions and behavioral traits deliberately to obtain what is desired. Manipulators use their ability to understand others and get what they want by using trickery, misdirection, persuasion, charm, and coaxing.

In the mind of a manipulator, he or she thinks, *I can change people's behavior and let them give me what I want.* Skilled manipulators can even come out of a situation when they get caught trying to use other people to their advantage.

A manipulator tends to create a certain level of strain in a situation. They use multiple techniques to mold their personality according to their goals. A manipulator can make you feel on top of the world or the worst person on this planet. It all depends on how that manipulator wants you to act.

Manipulation, as a concept, involves two parties. One is the manipulator, and the other is manipulated. While manipulators are extremely aware of their surroundings, some personalities tend to ignore that. People who are emotionally vulnerable or don't have a clear mindset tend to get manipulated.

Generally speaking, everyone manipulates without knowing. Lying or hiding the complete story are two common ways of manipulation; however, manipulators live these tactics as a way of life. They use various tactics as their tools to fool you into doing what they want.

That's why you need to understand all types of manipulation and, more importantly, learn how to address it positively in different aspects of your life.

Chapter 2: How Manipulation Works

When you are manipulating a person, you start with a step known as "analysis". This is where you use the practice of analyzing a person's behavior, personality, attitude, vocabulary, and voice practices to learn more about who they are. This enables you to personalize your strategy specifically to what drives and encourages that person to think or feel in a specific way. It is important that you complete this step as you will have greater success bypassing their conscious desire for fight or flight in uncomfortable situations and, instead, learn to make them feel more comfortable and confident around you. Then, you can use this comfort and confidence to help them see why saying yes to your offer or request would be more valuable than saying no.

Manipulation is part of the overall process. This comes later in the conversation after you have already persuaded someone to see why you are a trustworthy and genuine person. You use manipulation strategies to help you know how to effectively word something so that people are more inclined to say yes to what you want them to say yes to, rather than simply saying no to anything you ask or offer to them.

Persuasion starts before manipulation happens, but it lasts well after manipulation has taken place too. Persuasion is the practice where you create a sense of similarity and relatability between yourself and your target. This is your opportunity to help them see why you are trustworthy and genuine and to help build rapport between yourself and them. Then, once you have made your request using manipulation tactics, you can use persuasion to help encourage the person to see why you are right and why they should agree with what you have asked or offered.

Manipulation can be used in many different forms. You can use it when you are shopping or in business to negotiate better deals. You can use it when you are making sales to encourage a greater return on your sales. It can be used when you are looking to get something for free, borrow something, or otherwise have a favor granted or really at any other time. Manipulation is a powerful tool that can make it effortless to get what you want.

Different Types of Manipulation

If you aren't aware enough, manipulators can use many techniques to control you. They change their approach depending on the victim's personality, so they first observe you and learn your core personality traits. At the core, you can be a loving person, a lonely person, naive, or too confident.

With personality observation, manipulators create their tactic to attack you. Here are different types of manipulation that you need to become aware of:

1. Hiding the complete story

You can notice this in your office, parties, and other conversations taking place around you. Some people hide certain portions of stories to create a diversion. The listener of the story gets to know what the manipulator wants him or her to know.

What if a colleague in your office tells you how others are bitching about you! It is possible that you are getting half of the side of the story, but if you are unaware of manipulation, this half story can trigger emotions like anger and hatred, and you end up doing something that you regret.

When a manipulator uses a half story, they don't lie; they just avoid telling certain portions so that you see a picture of their creation. The tactic behind this method is to stay on the safe side. If exposed, the manipulator can simply say that he or she has explained nothing but the truth, and in doing so, you risk facing humiliation because of your wrong actions.

2. Lying

Generally, people lie when they are scared or want to get out of an unwanted situation, but a manipulator's lie is different. Their lies always have a purpose or an end goal. They don't even have to plan before lying. They can plan their next lie while having a conversation with you.

Depending on what they want, manipulators can choose different lies to make you their victim. It is a blend of thrill and excitement they feel while trying to play your personality.

3. Love and charm

Narcissistic manipulators use love and charm to control you. This behavior is majorly visible in love relationships between partners. You get hooked and think that your partner loves you the most. They charm and create an illusion of a perfect relationship. These people always want something from you.

When love has built the foundation, the manipulator uses that to control you. They can ask for things or money or just play with your emotions. The goals depend on the personality of the manipulator. Some people have the disorder to love and then hurt their partners.

The roots of this behavior lead back to their own previous experiences.

To spot the manipulation of love, you need to notice who is making decisions in your relationship:

- Do you feel nervous about your partner when making a personal choice?

- Has it become your habit to get your partner's approval on everything?

- Are you doing things that you wouldn't do otherwise?

These questions can help you decipher love manipulation in your daily life.

4. Changing behavior frequently

This is different from changing personality traits according to a victim. A manipulator, many times, may showcase a behavioral change toward the same person again and again. Now, you can think of all those people who seem different every time you meet them. This behavior is common in love relationships and boss-and-employee relationships as well.

The manipulator wants you to stay malleable and out of balance, so one minute he or she can look happy, and the next, swiftly become angry for no valid reason. However, they make you think that their behavioral switch has a legitimate reason. Your boss can start shouting angrily just for a single typo in your report. Similarly, a manipulative partner can come home with a different mood every day.

We, as humans, understand other people's personalities before socializing. You feel more comfortable around a person whom you know well, instead of a stranger, but manipulators use their mood swings to keep you scared and afraid of them. You feel unaware of their personalities and try to please them.

5. Denying accusations

A manipulator can deny things very impressively. If you accuse them of something, they confidently present a believable story. The confidence, combined with an impressive story, makes you believe them.

Denying accusations is the simplest form of manipulation. This is the first tactic that manipulators use in their early ages. A kid with manipulative tendencies usually denies things with confidence and makes stories to justify their case.

6. Punishments

Punishment is a disciplinary action to control other people's behavior. This is also a manipulation technique that gives your control to a manipulator. Physical violence, shouting, and nagging are visible techniques of manipulation.

Apart from that, you can also get emotionally punished with the silence of a person or mental abuse. A manipulator can attack your emotional vulnerabilities to make you feel bad. They keep on doing it until you start behaving the way they want. Such manipulation is seen in marriages a lot. One partner uses physical and mental abuse to control the other. Also, you can notice these manipulation symptoms in a parent-kid relationship. A manipulative kid can use the silent treatment to control his or her mother.

7. Blaming for overreaction

Is there a person who makes you feel bad about yourself? That person can be a manipulator.

Using the blame game allows a manipulator to put you on the faulty side of every conversation. If you point out their actions, they blame you for overreacting. They say that you are reacting way too much for a very small thing. This way they become the victim, and you end up feeling bad about your actions.

8. Victim targeting

You are the victim, but the accuser makes you defend yourself in front of others. This way, the manipulator masks his or her wrongdoings by shifting the focus toward you. The manipulator does it all in front of you, but you feel out of control of the situation.

9. Playing a victim

Have you ever helped people whom you never liked as a person? Then it is possible that you were used with this manipulation technique.

Manipulators play victim from time to time to gain compassion and sympathy. Their end goal is always to use you in some way; however, not every victim is a manipulator. Some are genuinely hurt and require your support, but manipulators can use your helping nature to get what they want.

10. Too much positive attention

The corporate world is filled with such manipulators nowadays. People use expensive presents, give money, and praise to lure you toward them. Excessive charm and too much attention are used for people who seek approval and like getting praised. Manipulators judge personalities and give too much attention to satisfy your emotional needs.

Positive attention works if you are emotionally vulnerable. For instance, if you mention "society" before taking every action, it tells a manipulator about your approval-seeking nature. Your high-class dressing sense and money-focused behavior also give signals to manipulators. They start giving you the royal treatment and manipulate in the process.

11. Diversions

Shifting situations and conversations are also manipulation techniques. You feel you know what's going on, but suddenly, a person changes the whole picture. If that happens in your life frequently, then there is a manipulator around you. He or she wants you to stay confused while they get to twist situations in their favor.

When in a group conversation, a manipulator plays the role of a narrator. If a conversation goes against his or her plan, they immediately shift the topic to something else. These manipulators become the kings and queens of office politics.

12. Isolation

Manipulation is difficult when you are consulting your family and friends on the same topic; hence, a manipulator tries everything to isolate you from other people. This doesn't have to be literal isolation. The manipulator can tell you to keep things a secret from everyone. Once you agree to that, he or she can twist your behavior easily.

Being able to manipulate someone's thoughts is not as difficult as you may suspect, and it can have a powerful effect on your ability to get them to think in the way that you want them to think so that you can have your desired outcome.

There are seven general ways that people can manipulate others. Unlike persuasion, these are not techniques that you use necessarily in conversation, such as anchoring or pacing. Rather, these are other important techniques that are involved in the relationship you build with a person you are talking to and how you can use that relationship to manipulate them to have certain thoughts and decisions that work in your favor. The following strategies are an important part of the manipulation:

1. Trust

Having the trust of the people you are talking to is important. When people trust you, they are much more likely to listen to you. They will feel more compelled to have conversations with you, they will be more likely to respect what you say, and they will be more likely to agree with you or comply with you when you exercise authority.

Gaining trust in your relationship comes from using tactics such as mirroring, as well as by generally being trustworthy. Show that you genuinely care about what they are saying and that you have an interest in their wellbeing. Make them feel as though they can feel confident in your ability to think for their better interest so that they don't have to when they are with you. This way, when you make a request, suggestion, or subliminal command, they are much more likely to comply because they know you think with their best interest at heart.

2. Secret hypnosis

Secretly hypnotizing people without them knowing it is a powerful form of manipulation. Technically, you achieve this by using persuasion techniques such as pacing and anchoring. The reason we mention this under the manipulation position is that it is important and relevant in both strategies. If you want to successfully persuade and manipulate people to do what you want them to do, you need to be able to hypnotize them secretly. This is also relevant and important for deception and particularly subliminal messages

When you have people under secret hypnosis, you can speak directly to their subconscious, and you don't have to worry about their conscious mind getting in the way. While you do still need to accommodate their conscious mind in the conversation, you have a direct passage to their subconscious mind to help activate your mind control strategies. It is important to understand how important this process is and activate it in every conversation when you want to be in control.

3. Authority

People are naturally more inclined to comply with someone who speaks and acts with authority, instead of someone who appears to be intimidated or uncertain about what they are saying. If you are uncertain, waiver in your stance, or otherwise appear to be underconfident, people are going to pick up on this and will feel less compelled to listen to you. They do not like to follow those who are not confident and strong. This could potentially lead them into a situation they don't want to be in. However, if you are leading with authority through confidence, strength, and certainty, people are going to assume that you know what you are talking about and they will feel more inclined to listen and comply.

Manipulation works heavily through knowing how to assert yourself in a conversation and use a human's nature against them. By understanding how people naturally behave, act, and think, you can use this to your advantage and create a situation that will allow you to carry the control in the conversation and manipulate people's thoughts and feelings to work in your favor.

4. Proof of results

People have always been more likely to act when there is proof that the results are what they are looking for. This is why having proof of the results they can expect when doing what you say will be extremely helpful in getting your way. Think about it this way: humans are herd animals; we do not like to be left behind or feel as though we are the odd one out. If you have proof that others have done it, then the people you are talking to are going to want to be one of those people too. They will not want to be left out or feel as though they are the only ones not doing it, so they will naturally feel infinitely more inclined because they want to follow the herd.

Chapter 3: Why Manipulators Manipulate

Now that you are fairly competent in identifying emotional and covert manipulation tactics let's understand what leads people to manipulate others. This may help you deal with them more efficiently.

We've all been victims of everything from pathological lying to being made to feel inadequate to suffering awful smear campaigns. They are beyond reasonable standards of human behavior. What makes people turn into sinister manipulators? What leads manipulators to use the tactics they do? What makes them defy norms of human behavior and turn to underhanded techniques to have their way with people?

Read on to get deeper insights about what makes people manipulate others in ways you'd never imagine.

Fear

Why does a person use manipulation to fulfill his/her agenda? Simple—fear!

It is obvious that manipulators fear that they will never be able to gain the desired outcome on their abilities. That if they act ethically, people and life will not reward them positively. They operate from the view that people are living, and people are positioned against them. Manipulators fear everyone as their enemy and believe life will not necessarily be favorable to them if they act favorably.

There is a fear that resources are limited, and if they don't gain something, others will. They think it's a dog-eat-dog universe where people must be controlled to help them accomplish the desired result. This control can be in any form—emotional, psychological, financial, or practical. They want to control people, so they can achieve their desired agenda and put their fear to rest.

Manipulators are constantly living under fear and insecurity. "What if this doesn't happen?" "What if my partner leaves me for someone else?" "What if someone gains the upper hand over me?" They want to win and control all the time to combat an inherent sense of fear.

Where does this fear stem from? It originates from a deep sense of unworthiness. This simply translates as "I am certainly not worthy of the good things and people in life. Hence, these things and people will leave me. To prevent them from leaving me, I must resort to some underhanded techniques that will give me absolute control over the people and things I believe I don't deserve." In short, the underlying message is, "I am undeserving or unworthy of people and things!"

Low or No Conscience

Lack of conscience is another fundamental reason for manipulation. When a person fails to realize that he/she is responsible for their reality, there is a greater tendency to operate without a conscience. Manipulators don't believe a fair system exists. Also, they've stopped evolving. They don't learn from earlier experiences or try to accomplish a state of congruence between inner emotions and eternal life.

They view manipulation as a safe or secure world for getting the desired result, despite the fact that these results have not satisfied them in the past. Emotionally and psychologically, they keep coming back to square one from time to time, never learning their lesson. To avoid this lesson, they will create another reason to manipulate. Thus, they are caught in a vicious circle of unworthiness or dissatisfaction, thus creating another manipulation need.

Manipulation doesn't pay beyond the initial brief fix since the manipulative action is not authentic, balanced or effective. It is a defense reaction to perceived hurt, unworthiness, fear, or insecurity. By being manipulative, the person is attempting to offset these emotions.

Manipulation is a deliberate act that is not aligned with a person's conscience or the greater good. The person doesn't operate with a "we are one" understanding, which means he/she seeks to gain through manipulation by authenticity rather than nonauthenticity. Anything gained through nonauthenticity only leads to narrow victories, ongoing trouble, emptiness, or fear, and unworthiness. This creates an even greater sense of unworthiness. Again, unworthiness is a fear of not being worthy of others' love and acceptance.

Manipulative folks do not learn, evolve, or realize the power of authenticity. Lack of realization of the real power of authenticity and worthiness comes from knowing that one is cherished and accepted for what they are. In essence, a feeling of unworthiness is often at the core of manipulation.

They Don't Want to Pay the Price Attached to Reach Their Goals

People often manipulate to serve their needs because they do not want to pay the price attached to their goal. They often strive to accomplish the objective or serve their purpose without wanting to give back or pay the price in return.

For instance, if you don't want your partner to leave you, the relationship will take work. You'll have to give your partner love, compassion, understanding, time, loyalty, encouragement, inspiration, a secure future, and much more.

A manipulator may not want his/her partner to leave them, but they don't want to pay the price of maintaining a happy, secure, and healthy relationship, whereby the partner will never leave them. They may not want to be loyal or spend much time with their partner, yet they expect them to stay. When people are not ready to pay the price of accomplishing what they want, they may resort to manipulation or underhanded techniques to achieve these goals without paying the price attached to them.

Similarly, if a manipulative person wants to be promoted in his/her workplace, rather than working hard, staying past work hours, upgrading their skills, or getting a degree, they will simply manipulate their way into the position. The person is not prepared to pay the price or do what it takes to be promoted.

At times, it's deeply ingrained in a person's psyche that wants are bad or that he/she shouldn't have any desires since it makes them come across as selfish. Manipulation then becomes a way to get what they desire or need without even asking for it.

Manipulators realize there is a price attached to everything. A person won't do them a favor without expecting a favor in return. They won't keep getting things if they don't demonstrate kindness and gratitude. A person won't love them or have sex with them without getting commitment, loyalty, and love in return. Manipulators try to push their luck by trying to get something without paying the price attached to it. It is often an easy way out.

They Think They Won't Get Caught

Another reason people manipulate is that they think they can get away with their sneaky acts and that the victims won't realize they are being manipulated. They are also confident that the victim can't do anything even if their manipulation cover is blown.

What gives manipulators the feeling that they won't be caught? Some people come across as inherently clueless, vulnerable, insecure, and naive. These are the type of people manipulators prey on. They believe a person who has low confidence, a low sense of self-worth, or is clueless about the ways of the world is less likely to figure out that he/she is being manipulated.

Also, manipulators know that if their manipulation cover is blown, the victim will not be able to do much. They cleverly pick targets who are low in confidence, self-acceptance, body image, or sense of self-worth. It is easier to play on the vulnerabilities of these people than on assertive and self-assured people who won't allow people to take advantage of them.

For example, say a person has low awareness of social dynamics, doesn't understand jokes easily, doesn't identify a prank early, is unable to differentiate between genuine courtesy and sexual advances, can't tell when someone is genuinely attracted to them, or simply wants to go to bed with them and other similar social and interpersonal dynamics—that person is more likely to be manipulated.

Manipulators are well aware that their victims can't do anything if they don't even realize that their weaknesses are being misused. They often cash in on the cluelessness of their victims by saying they are imagining things or making something up. An already clueless and unsure person is less likely to question this idea. When you are already reeling under feelings of insecurity, cluelessness, and vulnerability, how difficult is it for a manipulator to take advantage of these feelings by reinforcing them further?

Manipulators

Manipulators manipulate because they think they can hurt or upset their victims more than the victims can hurt or upset them. They will almost always target people who come across as nice and vulnerable. When people are oblivious to the dishonesty existing within social relationships, they aren't really accustomed to dishonest allegiances. This doesn't equip them with the means to confront or counter dishonesty, which makes them less aware of being manipulated.

They Aren't Able to Accept Their Shortcomings

When people are unable to come to terms with their shortcomings or do not accept the responsibility or accountability for their faults, there is an inherent need to make others feel lesser than them.

If manipulators aren't good enough or feel miserable about themselves, there is a desire to make others feel equally worthless or miserable about themselves. When a person believes he/she is unworthy of someone, they will manipulate the person to feel unworthy too. They can then gain control over his/her perception that they need the manipulator in their life to feel worthy. By putting others down or gaining control over others, they experience a form of pseudo-superiority. If they can't be good enough for others, they make others feel like they aren't good enough to retain control over them.

In effect, manipulators don't want their victims to realize that they (the manipulators) aren't good enough or unworthy of them (the victims). The manipulator will therefore carefully cultivate a feeling of helplessness and unworthiness within the victim to keep them hooked to him/her. If a person realizes that he/she is more attractive, intelligent, richer, capable, efficient, self-sufficient, etc., the higher their chances will be of leaving the manipulator. On the other hand, if the manipulator injects a feeling of the person not being "complete", they'll need someone to "complete" them.

Manipulators cannot accept their shortcomings or deal with criticism. They are often grappling with deep psychological issues or insecurities. By manipulating others, they do not have to confront their insecurities to feel higher than others. For someone operating with such a narrow perspective, even a little correction, feedback, or criticism can seem like a huge defeat.

People who manipulate don't know how to deal with defeat. When you hesitate to give feedback because the person will get defensive or blow things out of proportion or won't take things in the right spirit, it may be a sign you are dealing with someone who can't come to terms with criticism.

Notice how manipulators will seldom express feelings of gratitude or thankfulness. They find it challenging to be grateful to others because, in their view, by doing so they are increasing their sense of being obligated to another person, which doesn't give them an upper hand in any relationship.

For example, if you do someone a huge favor, they feel obliged to return that favor, which puts you above them in the relationship dynamics until they return the favor. Manipulators don't want to give you the upper hand by feeling obliged to you. Therefore, they will demonstrate minimal gratefulness, so you don't believe you've done something huge for them or that they are obliged to you. The idea is to always be one-up on you, and this feeling of being indebted to you doesn't make them feel one up.

Chapter 4: Analysis Techniques

Analysis techniques are simple observation techniques that you can use on a whim to get a sense of who someone is and what they are thinking at any given time. This is your golden chance to get a feel for a person's personality and really understand what types of things would drive them to make various decisions. You are then going to use this information later when it comes to manipulation. Because of how helpful this information is, it is important that you be sure to analyze as effectively as you can. In some situations, you may not have much time to analyze a person. In others, you may have ample time. Either way, the following strategies are excellent for helping you get a sense of who someone is and what you need to do to get what you want or need from them.

Analysis can take days, or it can take minutes. If you are trying to analyze your boss at work to get a feel for what you need to do to get a raise, for example, you might find that you have ample time to get a sense of who they are and what is required for them to make a decision. Alternatively, if you want to negotiate a sale or get a better deal if you are the one buying, you may not have terribly long to invest in analyzing. For that reason, it is important that you know how you can use simple and effective strategies that give you answers quickly. Then, if you do find that you have ample timing, you can continually use these skills to build confidence in your answers to ensure that you are well-informed before you approach someone for any given reason. If you are ready to learn about simple and effective analysis strategies, let's get started.

Profiling a Person

Profiling a person is the practice of getting to know everything you can about a person merely based on looks. You get the opportunity to get a sense of who they are and how they feel about themselves, as well as how they interact with others. If you are lucky, you may even get to see them making decisions when talking to those that they are surrounded by so that you can get a sense of what drives them to make decisions in their lives. There are three ways that you profile a person. This can be done in as little as a few minutes and can give you information right away. You start by looking at their environment, then at them, and then at the people they are surrounded by. This will give you an idea of what they think of themselves, who they think they are, and who they actually are.

What Their Environment Looks Like

You want to start by getting a sense of what a person's environment looks like and how they carry themselves in the environment. Environments can mean everything. For example, the same people who are spending time in expensive restaurants and upscale venues are not also spending their time at cheap bars or hanging out on a sidewalk smoking cigarettes with their friends. You can tell so much about who a person is and how they spend their time based on the environment they are in. It is important that you not only assess the environment, however, but that you also assess how comfortable they feel in it. This will give you the opportunity to get a sense of whether or not they actually spend much time in these environments or if they actually feel as though these environments reflect who they are as a person.

For example, if you see people regularly spending time in upscale restaurants and venues and they are completely confident in these environments, you know that they are confident in their social status and see themselves as a part of high-class society. If, however, they are in the same environments, but they act as though they are out of place or seem to have a great amount of insecurity and show it in how they carry themselves, you know that they do not view themselves as a part of high-class society. Instead, they are there for some other reason. At that point, you would want to find out what that other reason was as that reason would be something they care about greatly, whether it be money, a partner, a friend, their family, or otherwise.

The same goes for virtually anywhere. If a person is regularly attending and feeling confident in poetry slams, paint classes, acting classes, and otherwise, you know that they are likely an artistic type and that they highly value self-expression and creativity. If they are hanging out in family restaurants and venues with their spouse and children all the time, you know that they are most comfortable in family environments and that they hold their family in a very high and important position in their life. You can conclude a lot from a person's environment.

What They Look Like

Next, you want to pay attention to what the person looks like. You want to consider both the clothes they are wearing and their grooming. You also want to consider how comfortable they feel with both of these things.

To make it simple, start with their clothes. Do their clothes fit the venue that they are in? Do they look as though they are dressed the same as others around them, or are they dressed in a way that doesn't seem to fit in properly? For example, are they at a high-class venue wearing jeans and a T-shirt? Or are they at a sports bar wearing a glamorous dress and high-heeled shoes? If they are dressed in a way that doesn't seem to fit in with the environment they are currently in, it would suggest that they are not commonly found in this environment and that it is new and therefore out of place for them. You would then want to pay attention once again to who they are with or what is drawing them to the environment as this will teach you more about what they genuinely care about.

Next, look at their grooming. How is their hair? Is it freshly cut and styled, or is it messy and overgrown? Are they wearing any makeup? If so, how well put on is it? Does it look like they have experience, or does it look fairly thrown on? Then, look at other clues that would suggest their grooming habits. Are they freshly bathed? Do they smell nice – if you can tell from where you are? Are their nails well maintained? You want to pay attention to as many aspects of their grooming as you can. How a person grooms themselves directly relates to how they feel about themselves. A person who is well groomed and well maintained tends to feel better and more confident about themselves than a person who is not. The more attention a person gives to this aspect of their appearance, the more you can tell about how they feel about themselves. Furthermore, compare their grooming to those around them. If they are better groomed than those in their surroundings, that may mean that they have a higher sense of self-confidence or self-assurance than those around them. If their grooming standards are lower than the people around them, it may mean that they lack self-confidence and self-assurance and that they have "given up" on themselves.

Finally, look at their comfort in how they are dressed or groomed. When people are dressed or groomed in a way that is natural to them, and they feel good about it, they will wear it with confidence. This means that they will stand taller, walk with conviction, and will fidget minimally. If their present appearance is not normal for them or they are unhappy with how they look, they will regularly fuss with their appearance. They may play with their hair more as though they are trying to obsessively fix it, pull at their clothes, or walk unsteadily in their shoes. They may also try and physically shrink themselves by slouching, hiding behind the people they trust in the environment, and otherwise trying to make themselves "disappear physically". People who are doing this are either uncomfortable in their environment and have been drawn there by someone or something that they deem important, or are uncomfortable in a sense that they are not typically in such environments, so whether they are enjoying themselves or not, they currently feel like they don't fit in.

Whom They Surround Themselves With

Lastly, you want to look at whom the person is surrounded by. What are the noticeable behavioral patterns that you notice about that person and the people they are with? Are they noisy or reserved? Are they jokesters or serious? Do they keep to themselves, or are they outgoing? Are they drinking the spiked punch or not? You want to pay attention to as much as you can about the entire group.

The reason the group is so important is that people befriend the people that they feel are most like them. As a result, despite the individuals in a group being unique, the group overall will possess very similar qualities in many ways. You can watch the group and see what the common traits are as an opportunity to get an idea of what a person feels about themselves. This will be more honest than what they try and tell you based on where they are and how they are dressed. People will often make themselves up in their environment and their appearance, regardless of whether or not it is true to them. However, when they are surrounded by people they are comfortable around, they will—virtually always, without a doubt—act exactly as they are. This means that you will get to see the "unfiltered" version of themselves. And since you will then have a group of people to watch, you get a greater opportunity to understand many aspects of that person.

Finally, in addition to seeing how the specific person you are analyzing carries themselves, see how they act toward the other people around them. For example, if the group is typically quiet and reserved, but they encounter someone who is louder and more outgoing, what is the natural reaction of the person you are analyzing? Do they seem comfortable around the louder and more outgoing personality type, or does it make them uncomfortable or even angry? Getting to know how a person interacts with others, especially those they are less comfortable around, is a great way to know how they will interact with people they trust less or whom they don't already have a great connection with—namely, you.

Reading Basic Body Language

The next step of a simple and effective analysis is reading basic body language. This is a quick and easy step, and it takes only a few seconds. This is where you are going to get to use basic body language and a small mixture of common sense to generate a quick and basic idea of how a person is feeling or what they are thinking in any given moment. You may likely know many of these signals, but in case you don't, we are going to review them quickly. This will ensure that you are well prepared for anything.

The idea of reading basic body language is that you want to get a sense of the four ways that people tend to carry themselves. The first way would be as though their entire stature is lifted upward and toward the sky. Their back is straight, their shoulders are tall, their head is level with the ground, and they seem to be "lifted" almost as though there is a very light gravitational pull directly above them that pulls them "up". This type of body language signifies confidence. This person is both confident in their environment and themselves. They likely have few insecurities about who they are, and therefore, they tend to have a strong sense of self. They are less likely to be shaken by fear or sadness and more likely to respond well to empowering words of motivation.

Now imagine that same gravitational pull goes behind a person and lightly pulls them backward. Their cheeks are pulled back toward their ears, their shoulders are slouched backward, and their arm may cross across their chest and hold it almost as though they are physically holding themselves backward, and they may even literally take a step or two back. These are all signals of a person who is feeling nervousness or fear. The pulling back is their subconscious "flight mode" kicking into action and making them feel as though they want to flee the scene at any given moment.

Next, imagine the gravitational pull goes below the person and is pulling them even further down than natural gravity already does. This person would likely be slumped downward with their shoulders drooping, their cheeks and eyebrows may be drooping, and their limbs are likely hanging loosely toward the ground. There is not much motion or movement in them; they are very low and sunken in their stance and how they carry themselves. This would imply that the person is literally feeling "down". They are sad, upset, or even feeling defeat about something.

Finally, imagine the gravitational pull goes in front of a person. This person may be loud and bold with their voice, make large gestures and actions with their body, and everything about them seems to be pressed forward. In this case, it may signify that they are an extrovert with a very outgoing personality. However, if they also have their face pushed forward, such as with their lips pursed and their eyebrows sewn together, this would indicate that they are feeling angry and aggressive. They are unhappy and are openly expressing it.

These are the most basic types of body language. To get a sense of how someone is feeling overall, take a look at them, and place an imaginary gravitational pull on them where it appears like they are being pulled toward. This will help you determine which overall mood they are presently feeling.

Reading Complex Body Language

In addition to using someone's body language to determine what their mood is, you can also use it to determine what they are thinking. People's body language can tell you what they think if you know what to look for. To keep this simple and effective, we are only going to look at two fundamental aspects of complex body language: the hands and the feet.

Begin by looking at someone's hands. When you are analyzing their hands, you are looking for three things: placement, movement, and grip strength. Where their hand is placed will tell you what they are thinking. For example, if their hand is on their lap, this means they are relaxed, but if their hands are folded on their lap, it means they feel submissive toward the person in front of them. If their hands are touching an object, you can determine what they are thinking based off of the object. For example, if they bring a purse with them and never take their hands off of it, you know that they think they are in an unsafe and untrustworthy environment. If they take their hands off of their purse and later place it back on their purse and don't immediately begin looking for something within it, then you know that they are getting ready to leave and their body is physically getting ready as they verbally prepare to exit the conversation they are having.

Next, the movement in their hand says a lot. For example, say their hand is placed on their lap, and they are rubbing their thumb back and forth over their leg, or one thumb back and forth over the back of the other hand. This would suggest that they are literally trying to caress themselves so that they can develop a sense of comfort. They are not feeling comfortable or confident in their environment, and they are trying to console themselves literally. If, however, they were fidgeting, such as by grabbing at a piece of their clothing or shaking something around, it would suggest that they were either bored or nervous. A completely neutral body language that is void of emotion combined with fidgeting would symbolize boredom, whereas a pulled back body language with fidgeting would symbolize fear. If they were pulled down showing that they were sad and they were fidgeting, it would symbolize that they were thinking about what was making them upset.

Lastly, you want to consider what grip their hands presently have on whatever they are holding. A light grip suggests that they are feeling comfortable or maybe even submissive in their environment. A mild or medium grip would suggest that they are confident in their environment but that whatever message you are gaining from what they are presently gripping (e.g., their purse) would symbolize that they are feeling pressured about that message and it is in the foreground of their mind. If their grip is extremely tight, it indicates that whichever emotion their overall body language is suggesting is being amplified and they are feeling that emotion to the extreme level.

Once you are done looking at the hands, you want to look to the feet. The feet will tell you two important things: what the person is thinking and what the person wants to do. If a person is fidgeting with their feet, such as by shaking their heel around or bouncing their foot, this would indicate that they have something on their mind. They may be nervous and wanting to leave, they may be waiting, or they may be eager to share a piece of information and are trying to diffuse their energy elsewhere as they cannot currently share what is on their mind. They may also be bored and trying to alleviate some of their boredom. Once again, you can determine this based on what they are presently doing with the rest of their body language and what their overall mood is.

Next, you want to pay attention to where their feet are pointing. The person or object that lies directly ahead of where their toe is pointing will tell you what a person wants to do. If their toe is pointing at the door, they want to leave. If it is pointing at a person, they are interested in that person. If it is pointing at the television, they are interested in the television. If it is pointing at the bar, they want to get a drink, and so forth. Whatever lies at the end of their toe tells you what a person is thinking about and what they want to be doing.

Understanding Tone of Voice

Lastly, you want to pay attention to the person's tone of voice. Their tone of voice will tell you a lot about what they feel directly in response to what you or anyone else has said to them and about how they feel about the topic at hand. You can hear much emotion in a person's voice, and this is, ultimately, what you want to be paying attention to. This, combined with their words, will give you a sense of how they feel about specific things. When you can put these two together, you can get a fairly strong sense of what they think about certain topics too.

Start by eavesdropping on a conversation that the person is having or begin one with them yourself. Then, listen to what their "baseline" is. This is their neutral emotion or how they talk when they are not emotionally engaged. This is where most people talk on a general basis. Then, you want to see if you can notice what their different emotions sound like when they begin talking. For example, can you identify surprise, shock, or concern in their voice? Can you recognize happiness, joy, or excitement? Can you recognize anger, accusation, or annoyance? Can you recognize sadness, disappointment, or despair? Can you recognize fear, uncertainty, or anxiety? Try and recognize as many different emotions as you can as you are talking with them. The more you can recognize before you even begin trying to manipulate them, the better. This will give you the best leverage when it comes to determining what they are feeling regarding anything you are saying to them and how you can use these feelings to maximize your persuasion and manipulation efforts.

Chapter 5: Dark Psychology

It's a bit of a well-kept secret that the ability to manipulate people is a useful tool. It's one of the reasons why businesspeople and politicians get and hold their positions. There comes a certain point in your life wherein completely turning off your emotions and being pragmatic is a skill you need to have. Nobody likes to discuss it because we have this societal fear of the reality that people can just be seen as a means to an end.

The late Steve Jobs was particularly renowned for his ability to work people's emotions and to say just the right thing that would get them to come around to his view. It was so strong that the people around him developed a term for it: the "reality distortion field," a phrase coined from a similar phenomenon in the *Star Trek* universe.

There are numerous historical instances of Steve Jobs taking advantage of his unique ability to get precisely what he wanted. One such instance was when Jobs, in the 1980s, was trying to get Pepsi CEO John Sculley to come to Apple. This exchange spawned a famous line that many know today: "Do you want to sell sugared water for the rest of your life, or do you want to come with me and change the world?"

Much can be said about his specific ability to charm and manipulate people, not the least of which was his deep understanding of what people wanted as well as what people wanted to hear. Add to this an understanding of subtle intimidation, power cues, and a large amount of passion and charisma, and you have a powerhouse who could get pretty much whatever he wanted.

How does all this apply to you? Well, you're reading this because you want to learn how to work with people from the inside out. You want to know how to say just the right thing to get what you need and how to manipulate people, such that you can bypass any obstacles, so they will do exactly what you want. If that's the case, then you've come to the right place.

The fact is that the mind is a relatively simple thing. While the brain is infinitely complex, the manifestations of the conscious mind are both resolute and easy to work with. Most people work in very obvious and predictable ways, such that if they're a "normal" person, you can rather easily figure out the best way to work with them in no time flat.

In the end, this is about using the concept of neuro-linguistic programming to its fullest to get what you want out of people. A more common term for this is "manipulation". However, the aim of neuro-linguistic programming is slightly different. Neuro-linguistic programming is more focused on the long-term shifting of attitudes where manipulation is more based on immediate gains. That isn't to say that neuro-linguistic programming isn't a form of manipulation though; it absolutely is.

When you hear the term "manipulation", you will probably have some sort of knee-jerk reaction like, "Wait, isn't manipulation wrong?" And to this question, there is no simple answer.

Manipulation isn't wrong; manipulation is simply a tool. How you use it can determine whether it's wrong or not. For example, an example of manipulation being objectively wrong is doing something that gets somebody terribly hurt. There are also some unspoken rules that you should never break. For example, while it's pretty easy to take advantage of the fact that somebody's parent is dying, actually doing so is a major ethical gray area.

If you stick to maintaining an ethical approach, then manipulation proves itself as a method of understanding people and knowing how to work with them so things will work out better for you. You can even use manipulation for good purposes. One such example is Steve Jobs yet again, who used his reality distortion field for good causes, such as when he would convince his employees that it was possible to do something that was more or less impossible, which in turn, would make them work harder for the end result and eventually lead to a new mark being set in technology.

We all know that psychology is the study and analysis of the human mind and human behavior. So what is dark psychology? It is the science and art of manipulating and controlling the human mind through various methods. Psychology is central to human interactions, thoughts, and actions, whereas dark psychology involves the use of tactics of persuasion, motivation, coercion, and manipulation to get what you want.

There is a phenomenon in this realm referred to as the dark psychology triad that consists of elements that help in detecting potential criminal behavior in people. The dark triad is a combination of traits including narcissism, Machiavellianism, and psychopathy. What are the characteristic features of each of these dark triad traits?

- *Narcissism.* It is related to lack of empathy, high levels of egotism, and grandiosity.

- *Machiavellianism.* People with this attitude have little or no sense of morality and ruthlessly employ manipulation and other tactics to exploit or deceive others.

- *Psychopathy.* These people come across as very charming and charismatic and deep down are highly impulsive, selfish, lack empathy, and are fairly remorseless.

Yes, it is true that none of us wants to be manipulated, yet it happens in our daily lives with unerring regularity, many times unwittingly. Additionally, we also use mind control and manipulation tactics to try and get what we want. Dark psychology involves studying the psychodynamics of people who prey on and victimize others to achieve their own ends.

Some people use dark psychology tactics knowingly and with the intention to cause harm to others and there are those who use or are prey to these tactics in unwitting ways. Moreover, it is a survival instinct in all living beings to be wary of our surroundings and use guile and deception to survive and thrive. Multiple studies prove this innate ability to victimize others.

Although we believe that we have control over our actions and reactions, under extreme pressure, it is very difficult to predict our behaviors, and there are high chances that many employ shady tactics to escape from these pressures. The following studies are examples of how human minds behave in unpredictable ways when compelled or sometimes even when they may not have needed such an extreme reaction.

Let us look at some of these experiments conducted in the '60s and '70s by psychologists. While controversies are surrounding the experiments and plausible rationalizations were provided in retrospect, it goes without doubt that the human mind can be very unpredictable and is capable of reaching out to its dark aspects with little or no provocation.

The "learner" was actually only an actor.

If the learner gave a wrong answer, the volunteers were told to give electric shocks by turning the "dial", which had labels ranging from mild pain to extreme pain to even fatal. The experimenter wearing a lab coat told the volunteers that they should continue to increase the intensity of the "electric shock" until the learner gave the right answer. The volunteers could hear the simulated screams of the learner from the other room. If the volunteer did not want to increase the intensity, then the experiment told them to continue employing the following statements:

- Please continue.

- The experiment needs you to go on.

- It is essential that you go on.

- You have no choice. You have to go on.

There were startling and disturbing outcomes from this rather controversial experiment. Despite hearing the simulated screams of extreme pain from the "learners", sixty-five percent of the volunteers turned the knob to "fatal". They did not even bother to ask about the health of the learner. Yet most of the volunteers said that they would have never behaved this way but did not find the wherewithal to stand up to a figure of authority (lab-coated experimenter). Dark psychology is easy to trigger, isn't it?

The most disturbing observation of these kinds of experiments was the fact that the volunteers were not even aware that they were being manipulated and delving into the dark aspects of their minds. Another study which proved the unconscious behavior under authority goes as follows:

A group of volunteers was asked to watch a screen in which a basketball game was going on. They were told to count the number of passes that took place between players wearing white shirts. At some point during the game, a person dressed in a gorilla costume walked onto the court. The participants were so engrossed in counting the number of passes that they did not even notice this aberration. Many participants swore that no such disturbance took place! They were unconsciously following the orders of the experimenter.

Another common dark psychology tactic is called "priming" in which people's behaviors can be changed without them even realizing it. For example, read this sentence, "The house was so old that it groaned, creaked, and struggled to stand on its shaky foundation." Now, suppose you were to stand up, chances are very high that you will unconsciously have taken care to do so at a slower pace than usual as you were just now "primed" for old age.

Politicians are known to use priming to change voting preferences based on the location of the booth. Like this, there are many studies which prove that accessing and employing the dark side of our minds is not just easy but can happen without us even being aware of it.

Moreover, these theories have been applied and checked repeatedly throughout the history of humankind, and dark psychology is an integral part of our minds. This is not the same as conspiracy theories. Dark psychology only represents the innate need and desire for humans to dominate over others who are weaker than themselves to achieve their own ends. Marketing advertisements are classic examples of manipulating the minds of the buyers and convincing them to buy the product, which they may or may not need.

Therefore, it makes sense to know, understand, and appreciate this aspect of our minds and use strategies and tips to "prime" our minds and those of others in ways that will result in win-win situations for all concerned stakeholders.

Chapter 6: The Six Scientific Principles of Persuasion

The topic of persuasion has been researched for more than sixty years as scientists seek to uncover what influences a person to say yes to something. The results that have risen from these scientific studies are rather surprising and have taught many people how they can influence others to say yes when they are asking for a specific request to be approved. From the position of the person who is not making the decision, it may seem easy to assume that one would weigh all the pros and cons of their decision before landing on their final answer. However, science has shown that there are actually some very basic things that play into how a person will decide to say either yes or no based on a few basic shortcuts. These shortcuts exist because we live in a world where there is a constant pile of information being dropped into our laps, and if we were to attempt to weigh out the pros and cons of every decision fully, we would never have time to decide anything. We would be overloaded with decisions to make and things to consider, and it would result in some serious setbacks, ultimately rendering this more rational-based decision-making style useless.

According to science, there are six scientific principles of persuasion. These are the only principles responsible for how people make decisions based on what we currently know. These principles have been scientifically proven by Robert B. Cialdini, psychology professor and author, in his book *Influence*. We are going to explore what these six principles are and how you can become consciously aware of them so that you can always stay in conscious control of your decision-making skills. Again, while most people will have no idea that these factors even come into play when you are making a decision, a select few people who dabble in Machiavellian practices will attempt to use these principles against you. Staying clearly aware of them will ensure that you are always consciously making decisions in your favor and that genuinely serve your highest good without being unknowingly manipulated by another person.

Reciprocity

The first principle that encourages people to say yes when they have been asked a question is reciprocity. If you have given someone something, they feel obliged to say yes to give you something back because they feel as though they owe you in one way or another. This is true even if you have offered them the said thing as a gift or without the intention of receiving anything back from them. The same goes in the opposite direction too. Any time someone gives you something or does something nice for you, you feel obligated to do something to reciprocate the said action.

A great way to understand how reciprocity works is to consider a study that was conducted in restaurants between waitstaff and their clients. This study proved that any time a waiter or waitress brings you some form of a gift along with the receipt, you are more likely to leave them a larger tip in exchange for the gift. While most people would believe that such a small act does not influence behavior at all, the reality is that it does. The study proved that a single mint offered at checkout increased tips by three percent, but when two mints were offered, the tips increased by fourteen percent. If the waiter or waitress was obvious about the offering of the mints, such as by offering one mint before leaving the table, then turning back and saying something like, "For you fine people, here's an extra mint!" the tip was increased by twenty-three percent.

Manipulative people can take advantage of this type of behavior by ensuring that it is obvious any time they offer you something or do something nice for you. In making it obvious or pointing it out, they know that you will feel subconsciously obligated to say yes when it comes time to return a favor for them, which they most definitely plan on cashing in on. Typically, they already know what they want from you before they even offer you the nice gift or act of kindness, making the entire thing a manipulative sham.

Scarcity

One big way that people can be manipulated through scarcity is something that high-quality brands use to secure higher sales numbers. People like to have something that is unique and that no one else has, so when they know something is scarce, they are more likely to want to have it. Manipulative people have been using this information to their knowledge for years, knowing that people want what others can't have. This is tied directly with the human behavior of feeling special and unique.

A great example of this in business is with Birken Bags. Birken Bags are a high-quality bag that cost tens of thousands of dollars to purchase because they are a fashion icon that represents power and status. You might wonder what makes a Birken bag so special and why anyone would be willing to pay tens of thousands of dollars for a purse, and the reasoning is simple. Only a few hundred bags are made every single year, and you have to be on a waiting list or a special list to purchase the bag. That's right, it's not a first-come-first-serve system, but instead, it is a most-loyal-best-served system with Birken. By making their bags scarce and making the purchasing process meaningful and special, this company can profit on the human desire to feel special and unique.

Authority

People want to be a part of something bigger than themselves, which means that they need to follow some form of leader or authoritative figure that guides them through the process of being a part of that "something bigger". One big way that manipulative people will manipulate others is through creating a sense of authority and leading people from that authoritative position. This is why people in the business world will lead with their credentials over any other information to establish a position of authority and immediately get others paying attention to them and subconsciously wanting to follow their directions.

For example, a study was done in a real estate company where realtors were able to increase their appointment bookings by twenty percent and their signed contracts by fifteen percent simply by introducing their agents as authoritative figures. Instead of saying, "Sandra is going to help you today," for example, they would say, "Meet Sandra. She is the head of our sales and has over twenty years' experience in selling homes." This simple change leads to a fairly healthy impact on their sales, proving that a simple persuasive technique could have a significant impact on a company's bottom line. The same goes for virtually anyone, though, as this persuasive principle is not restricted to sales. Any time someone establishes themselves as an expert, whether it be in a self-help industry, as a religious leader, or even simply in your group of friends, that person will always receive more promising results from their requests than anyone else.

Consistency

People require consistency when it comes to persuading them to say yes to something. When someone is exposed to something consistently, they are more likely to be interested in it and saying yes becomes easier as they feel familiar with the offer that they are receiving. For example, "they say" that the average person has to see a piece of marketing about the same company seven times before they recognize it, and up to or beyond fourteen times before they are willing to look into it and make a decision. That is unless the company itself approaches the individual first and creates the connection. In that case, other persuasive measures can be involved to quicken the process and increase the person's likelihood of saying yes.

When people are seeking to influence someone into agreeing with them, they will always try to expose them to the idea several times over before they ask for the said person to take advantage of the offer. Through this behavior, they increase their chances of receiving a positive response and making the sale, closing the deal or getting the favor they wanted.

Liking

If someone does not like someone or something, they will almost definitely say no the minute they are asked to make a decision regarding that person or thing. People do not like being involved with people or things that they do not like. It is as simple as that. So when someone tries to persuade someone into saying yes or agreeing upon something, they will almost always do so by first gaining the admiration and appreciation of the person. For example, a company will first seek to gain your admiration before attempting to sell to you because this way they know that you are more likely to do so.

An example of how effective the simple basis of liking someone or something is can be shown by a study that was done between MBA (Master of Business) students in two well-known business schools. In this study, one group of students entered negotiations with the rule that "time is money; get straight to business," whereas the other group entered negotiations on the premises of "exchanging personal information prior to negotiations to identify a similarity before you begin." In the group that valued time and money over personal connections, only fifty-five percent of the negotiations reached an agreement. In the group that valued personal connection first, ninety percent of the negotiations ended in a successful outcome that was agreed upon by both parties. The outcomes that were reached by those who had established personal connections were also calculated to be eighteen percent more valuable to both parties than those reached by the ones who were more focused on their exchange of time and money. If people are genuinely looking to persuade you into getting on their side and working in their favor, they are likely going to do so by starting on a personal connection and then working up from there.

Consensus

People will always look for a common consensus between others when they are uncertain about what decision they should make. By looking at the actions and behaviors of other people, they can determine whether or not they want to do something or engage in something based on what other people are doing and the results that they are experiencing. This is how peer to peer sales and social marketing work—by using the positive testimonies and the marketing offered by existing clients to encourage new clients to begin purchasing from them too.

A great example of this can be seen in the growing trend in social marketing strategies. For example, in the past ten years, being an "influencer" on social media has become a serious career path that can offer serious income to anyone who engages in this strategy. Essentially, those who are becoming influencers are simply marketing for other companies and are being paid to do so. However, they are successful in doing so because they generate a large following that trusts in them and believes in their opinions. Through this trust, they can leverage their name and increase the number of sales companies earn, which increases even further as their following goes ahead and purchases the endorsed product and agrees that it is a great product. Through this domino-effect marketing strategy, companies can increase their sales infinitely while also maximizing their brand awareness through social media with significantly less time and money invested in the marketing process.

Chapter 7: The Benefits of Learning about this Skill

Learning about manipulation both in its positive and negative forms is important for any human who wishes to function healthily. Using persuasion techniques from NLP studies can increase your ability to manipulate others and be more influential, in general ethically. Ethical manipulation is an important skill in life and can be used for influencing clients, members of your family, or colleagues at work. Anyone who learns about NLP, for this reason, will access useful and powerful abilities to help support the process of ethical manipulation and persuasion.

The Benefits of Knowing about Persuasion and Manipulation:

Mastering these skills and the fine art of ethical manipulation will give you new opportunities for increases in your sales numbers, getting to know important or influential figures, better self-esteem, and the ability to express yourself naturally and authentically. The art of persuasion is an important part of the theory of communication, and these methods help create and foster healthy relations on a community level, along with customer and employee relations. When you are good at employing the correct use of argumentation, it will lead to raises, promotions, and influential or powerful positions. Let's look at a few more benefits to this:

- *Rapport.* One important benefit to learning about ethical manipulation is using it to build rapport with others. Rapport is what helps us feel at ease with another person, feel the common ground, and look for qualities shared in common. It is necessary for all positive interactions and achieving goals that include other people. Essentially, this happens when you feel comfortable with someone, relate to them easily, and have a warm interaction with them. Rapport relies on seeing common ground between you and another person.

  It's an important aspect of persuasion and manipulation because people are much more likely to do favors for others, or simply agree with them, if they see that person as similar to themselves. Therefore, everyone who knows how to persuade others ethically is aware of building rapport. In this book, we will give you a few methods for doing this with many different types of people. No matter how different the person seems from you, it's possible to find common ground and build rapport if you simply know how.

- *Seeing the needs and wants of others.* When you are effective at persuading other people, or knowing how to read signs of them trying to persuade, you catch a glimpse into what they find the most important. In this way, you can understand humanity on a deeper level and use this information to get ahead in life. When you recognize others' wants and needs, not only do you better understand them as an individual, but you can become closer. This is what separates positive and negative manipulation.

- *Effective communication.* Rapport-building and recognizing the needs of others are foundations that can lead to effective communication. Effectively communicating is useful for countless reasons, among which are conflict resolution, getting ahead in your career, and resolving conflicts on a professional and personal level. Let's look at the example of building healthy relations with employees from your work. Talking to them about benefit decreases, or impending layoffs, along with other unpleasant company decisions, requires a certain level of savvy that can be gained using ethical manipulation techniques.

One method for doing this relies on reaching your listeners using logic and facts. You could, for example, show that if your business doesn't close down a certain property, the rest of your businesses will have to close down. The second method relies on the fact that your listeners are paying attention mostly on an emotional plane, rather than using logic. In situations like this, appealing to empathy by illustrating examples of families who will suffer as a result of not taking action is more effective.

- *Finding shared values with anyone.* There are times, in life, when we are forced to work along with or spend time with people who seem very different from us. When you are effective at persuasion and ethical manipulation, this becomes easy. You can simply find shared values with them, no matter how different they appear to be on the surface. This allows you access to the skills of lightening tension in tough situations or getting people to do you favors readily. People are more likely to help those whom they see as similar to them, meaning that knowing how to find similarities is a must for interpersonal relations.

- *Beating resistance.* Marketing depends entirely on the buying habits of consumers. One hard habit to beat is buyer resistance in consumers. Effectively persuading buyers means helping them to feel at ease with their choices while simultaneously improving your sales numbers. The main factor in doing this is displaying to the buyer your understanding of the hard choice they are facing. Letting them know that you are aware of how difficult the purchase is and understand their feelings can allow them to let their guard down.

This allows the buyer to see you more like a human. They may then make a purchase that benefits them and you, as the salesperson. This, of course, applies not just to sales but to interpersonal situations. Empathizing with another person is a great way to get them to open up, feel more comfortable, and become decisive about important choices.

- *Expressing yourself more effectively.* Skills in influence and positive manipulation help individuals express themselves authentically. Constructing sound arguments that people come to agree with creates and sustains self-assuredness and confidence. Arguments that use logic rely on facts, not just opinions. Even though a person might start with a certain idea or opinion, researching the situation or material will allow them a chance to give others important and valid data and information. Speakers who are truly powerful and influential use facts to support their arguments and use that information to prove that they are correct.

Techniques for Persuasion and Manipulation Skills

This book will go over many different techniques for this, but let's start with the following basics:

- *Mirroring.* This is one of the quickest ways to build rapport with someone you just met. You pay attention to their bodily movements, the tone of voice, and values and mirror them subtly. For example, if someone is standing with their arms crossed, do the same thing. If they are speaking excitedly and quickly, match their tone and pitch. This must be done in a very subtle way, or it will have the opposite effect you're hoping for. The reason this is so effective is that you can eventually have someone follow you to a conclusion or decision that you wish for them to reach.

- *Questioning.* Another technique for this is discovering what people need and want by asking questions. You do this to elicit their personal values and figure out what they think is most important in this world; then you can appeal to those values by aligning your idea, service, or product with what they find important.

- *Honesty.* This is a key difference in ethical manipulation and negative, selfish manipulation. Effective influence and persuasion rely on honesty and transparency. Real, genuine, positive persuasion does not attempt to fool the audience, but rather gives a grouping of facts and information that the audience can consider to make the best choice. Learning the skill of effective influence using solid communication techniques can drastically improve self-esteem levels, job performance, and chances of securing positions of leadership.

- *Influence and persuasion should always be used for helping others, rather than hurting them.* False information shouldn't be used or given, and if you have a good understanding of true ethical manipulation, it will never be necessary. There are many benefits to gain from learning about NLP, including an extreme increase in your persuasion abilities, which might be the most important social skill you could develop. Since NLP techniques are so valuable, that is what we'll be focusing on in much of this guide. This chapter was intended to illustrate how important this skill is, so hopefully, you now have a fuller understanding of the subject.

Chapter 8: Seven Laws of Human Behavior

Human behavior is a fairly complex thing, but eight laws typically drive it. These laws outline the motivations behind most people's behaviors and actions and what it is that they are trying to achieve from everything that they do. They also help determine whether or not someone will do something based on how it falls within the laws of their behavior. For example, humans are driven by their need to know why they should do something, not how. Therefore, if you are attempting to sell something to someone, you need to explain why they should be interested, not how it will change their lives. This allows the individual to understand what they will gain and why it will change their lives, and then they can consider how the process works later on.

Machiavellian people are highly intelligent, so they know exactly what the eight laws of human behavior are, even if they have never gone out of their way to learn such information. Through watching, testing, and paying attention, Machiavellian leaders know how to identify these traits in people and use them as a means to manipulate their behavior and get what they want.

In this chapter, we are going to explore the eight laws of human behavior and how they work, as well as how people with power use these behaviors as an opportunity to manipulate others and get their way, often without ever getting noticed for their manipulative behaviors. As you read through these laws of behavior, notice how they appear in your own life and where these laws have motivated you. Then, consider how they can be used against you. By understanding these points in your behavior and recognizing them as being vulnerable toward masterful manipulators, you can lead your life with a greater sense of self-awareness and avoid being duped by a manipulator, such as a Machiavellian leader.

Avoiding Accountability

People are known for being more than willing to accept recognition while avoiding responsibility. In doing so, they award themselves the opportunity to receive all the praise despite never having done anything to earn it. In most instances, the hard work was completed by others while they sat around and took credit anyway. We see this happen consistently all over the world, particularly with bosses and CEOs who rarely engage in the company work but take all the credit for the success that the company produces. This is not just a phenomenon among corporations; it is a common influencer behind many people's behaviors.

To take recognition of things that have been done despite never having done any of the work means that you get to feel good more often than not. Even among children, we frequently see one child accomplishing something and another child taking responsibility for the said accomplishments, such as during school group work. In these situations, the child is being motivated by the recognition but is pushing everyone else to do the work for them so that they do not actually have to do anything to receive the recognition. Often, this is not done with the desire to be malicious or deceptive, but instead, we allow it to happen because the process of being recognized feels good.

The chances are that you can easily recognize this behavior in your life for things that you have done. For example, maybe you started a new hobby or business venture and accepted the praises of those who said that you were brave and talented, but when it came time to see the hobby or venture through, you stopped putting in the effort, and everything fell apart. In situations like these, it can be easy to say that it was a lack of motivation or drive that resulted in you not seeing it through and you can naturally move on to the next thing and continue with your life. However, that is not always the case.

Manipulative people are known to use this as an opportunity to increase their personal gains at the expense of others around them. A famous case of this happening was in the interactions that took place between Thomas Edison and Nikola Tesla when electricity and other primitive electronic devices were being developed more than a hundred years ago. In this exchange, Edison had hired Tesla to work for him, requiring Tesla to work for eighteen hours a day to fulfill his job duties. At one point, Edison proposed that if Tesla were to redesign the Edison dynamos completely, then he would give Tesla $50,000. When Tesla successfully redesigned the model, Edison pointed out that Tesla did not understand American humor and, instead, offered him a small raise for his hard work. From there, Tesla attempted to introduce new, more efficient electricity models to Edison, but Edison completely disagreed with Tesla and did everything he could to sabotage Tesla's success.

Later, Tesla went on to pursue his passion and moved along to a new company with George Westinghouse, the owner of a Pittsburgh electricity company. There, Westinghouse completely funded Tesla's research and offered Tesla a royalty agreement that would secure him profits from future sales based on his successful research. When Tesla proved to be successful, Westinghouse took recognition for Tesla's successes and allowed everyone to believe that it was he who had successfully produced the new form of electricity.

These were not the only two cases where Machiavellianism sabotaged Tesla and his recognition for his hard work. Over the years, many people took patents filed by Tesla and developed their own systems and then took responsibility for everything, including the work that Tesla had contributed to their systems. A famous example is Guglielmo Marconi, who was long seen as the "father of radio" despite having gotten his templates from Tesla's breakthrough. In these circumstances, Tesla simply did not have the cunning wit or social intelligence of the others, which resulted in him being taken advantage of. It wasn't until recent years, long after Tesla's passing, that people began to realize that the true mastermind behind these developments was none other than Tesla himself.

The best way to protect yourself against being taken advantage of, in favor of someone else receiving your rightful recognition, is by taking pride in your work and taking accountability in your deals. If you agree to do something for someone, always cover your bases and ensure that there are no loopholes that could be used to dupe you out of your rewards. Never let someone else take advantage of you and always make sure that you protect your right to speak up and take responsibility for your work. If you find yourself being taken advantage of by someone, create the opportunity for you to terminate that connection so that you can surround yourself with people who are not manipulative and cruel. Do not fall for the charm of others, always get things in writing, and protect yourself even if it seems unnecessary. You never know when you may be taken advantage of by others. Remember, a Machiavellian or manipulative person rarely looks like a dangerous person until you are already too deep in their games.

Looking after Self-Interests

People are driven by their inner desires, not the desires of those around them. Even in instances where it seems like someone is being driven by someone else's desires, the underlying driving force is their desires or reasons. For example, say you knew a loved one who smoked, and you wanted them to stop smoking because you were afraid of losing them to cancer. If you were to spend each visit letting them know how dangerous smoking is and asking them to stop because you did not want to lose them, they would likely not quit smoking because this would not be meaningful enough to motivate them. Even though it is a genuine and kind cause, it simply isn't their reason. Therefore, they do not personally feel driven by it. However, if this same person was to fall ill and find that smoking was the primary cause of their illness and they wanted to overcome the illness, they may find this to be meaningful enough to cause them to quit smoking. The key difference here is that they are being driven by something that is meaningful to them personally, rather than something that is meaningful to you.

Often, if people try to do things that are meaningful to someone else but not to themselves, they will find themselves struggling to stay committed to such a cause. This is not because they do not care about those around them or the opinions of those around them, but because they are simply not motivated enough to change their behaviors. The same goes for virtually everyone. People do things for their own reasons, not for our reasons.

A Machiavellian leader or a manipulator will appeal to your personal interests by first trying to gain an understanding of what is valuable to you and what you care about in your life. Typically, most people have some fairly standard core values: family, happiness, financial freedom, and health. However, each person will have their own set of unique values too. A manipulator will expertly identify these values by listening to you speak and paying attention to what you speak most about, especially when you start exhibiting signs of passion or deep interest. Then, they will use these values to manipulate you to formulate your own reasons as to why you should behave in the way that they want you to behave.

The best way that you can avoid having someone manipulating you through your own sense of reason is to make sure that you develop your self-awareness and that you have a strong understanding of what truly matters to you and why. Any time someone presents you with options or a decision, always take your values into account and honestly consider what matters to you and which option will genuinely meet your needs. Always look at the long goal too. Most manipulators will attempt to manipulate you by assuming that you will only consider the immediate gain that you have and that you will fail to honestly consider the long-term consequences that you may face if you do not achieve said gains. By paying attention to what you stand to gain (or lose) in the future, you give yourself the opportunity to genuinely consider all the pros and cons of every decision and make a choice based on what fulfills your needs rather than what fulfills someone else's.

Being Stubborn

Another way that manipulators will use your reasoning to their advantage is by getting you on board with their beliefs knowing that you are unlikely to back out once you have said yes. Getting people to change their minds is much harder than getting them to make an initial decision—since most people stand by their initial judgment on something, even if the alternative or negative information is later presented. This is because staying in agreement with their original belief keeps them united with the group that they have now identified themselves as a part of. For example, if you are a Republican but find that your beliefs are better represented by the Democrats, you might continue to support Republicans, even if you realize that they do not represent your best interest because you do not want to lose your "group". Psychology has shown that staying connected to your chosen group stimulates the reward pathway in your brain. Likewise, attempting to remove yourself from your chosen group, even with the desire of joining a new group, can trigger the same responses that produce withdrawal symptoms. This means that your brain is literally wired to keep you in compliance with your original decision, even if you no longer believe in it the way that you once did. Changing your mind and choosing a new path, group, or label to identify yourself with ultimately requires you to be willing to suffer through those painful symptoms so that you can adjust your perspective and pick a new option.

A manipulative person will first use this information to their advantage by presenting you with selective information to get you on board with what they need you for. Typically, they will not tell you anything negative about the situation until after you have already agreed to support them or stand by them in their decision. Even then, a true Machiavellian person will only present you with minimal amounts of negative information. You are more likely to be blindsided by the negative parts later on than you are ever to hear them from the Machiavellian—unless they are a piece of necessary information.

Knowing that people who use Machiavellian power and manipulators will use your logic and reasoning in this way means that you can protect yourself by allowing permission for you to change your mind. If you find that you have been supporting someone and later discover that they are wrong or even bad, do not continue supporting them because you are afraid to admit that you know. Instead, allow yourself to be willing to admit to your mistake and educate yourself on how you can do better going forward. Being open and honest with yourself and reserving your right to change your mind means that you can hold yourself in a position where should you find yourself supporting a manipulator or a Machiavellian, you can stop and realign with someone or something that actually supports your values.

Making Emotional Decisions

People are driven by their emotions, not the facts. Although factual information is important to many people, most people will first make a decision based on their emotions and then will search out the necessary factual information to justify their decision. Many people use this information to their advantage when it comes to influencing other people's behaviors, especially in the corporate world. It is not uncommon for salespeople and corporate leaders to tell you exactly what you want to hear first, appealing to your emotions and encouraging you to feel good about making a decision. Then, they will follow up with facts that reinforce those emotions so that you truly stay on board with the decision and feel like it is the right one for you. In most cases, people will do very little when it comes to appealing to factual information unless those facts directly support your emotional decision-making. They know that if they can get you to agree to what they want emotionally or need from you, then you will produce the facts to justify your choice all on your own.

This type of manipulation is especially common in personal relationships, such as those shared between lovers, friends, or relatives. In these relationships, you tend to feel a deep emotional connection to the other person that leaves you continually searching for logical reasons to justify your desire to stay in the relationship, even if it is toxic to you. This is why many people find themselves feeling trapped in toxic or dangerous abusive relationships because their emotions work in favor of the abusive or toxic person and their logic continually seeks to support their decision to stay. Abusive people know this and often use this as a method to manipulate people into staying in relationships with them, even if the other person knows better. This is why even people who are not considered to be particularly vulnerable to abusive relationships can be roped in and victimized by the abuse: because no one is truly completely immune to this form of manipulation.

The best way that you can protect yourself against getting pulled into manipulative tactics through your emotions is by slowing down and critically thinking about anything you are engaging in when your initial interest was based on emotions. Any time you find yourself feeling emotionally charged to make a decision, especially if that decision sounds too good to be true, stop and give yourself a moment to think rationally and search for unbiased facts surrounding the decision that you are seeking to make. Honestly consider whether or not it is going to be a good decision for you and then make the decision based on your rational thinking, even if it feels challenging or uncomfortable. If it feels as though you honestly cannot do this, first seek to find the honest facts and then back up your facts by determining how your emotions will feel long term. For example, say you are afraid to end a toxic relationship because you are afraid that you will be alone and you will never experience happiness again. Realistically, this is untrue, and this is just your emotional mind attempting to control your logical one. By recognizing that you can surround yourself with positive people and feel a greater sense of happiness after terminating the toxic relationship (because you will have more energy to contribute to other relationships in your life), this becomes a much easier decision. Always seek to make your decisions in the most unbiased way possible, and be willing to look at the alternatives or the long-term game if you are struggling to make a decision that is truly going to support you in feeling your best.

Feeling in Control of Personal Lives

As a human, you never want to feel as though you have no control over your life or the decisions that you make. For this reason, you will avoid making decisions regarding anything where it feels like the true choice is not in your power. You may have noticed that any time you spent time with another human who was particularly controlling, you felt as though this person was not enjoyable to spend time with and you may have even terminated the relationship. This is because spending time with this person took away from your feeling of control and the experience overall was uncomfortable.

Staying in control feels good because it feels like freedom, and freedom is something that humans crave. We do not like to be restricted by the feelings of pressure or feel we are no longer able to make our own decisions. These types of feelings can provoke fear and discomfort. This is why the entire Western world is built on the concept of "freedom". Realistically, we are not free, but we feel as though we are because we have the power to make many of our life decisions, such as where we will work, where we will live, and whom we will marry.

If we were truly free, we would be able to do anything without experiencing any repercussions from our decisions. Naturally, this would have serious consequences. In a truly free society, someone could commit a serious crime and never be held accountable for their actions because they had the freedom to behave in such a way. So countries with a democracy produce a sensation of freedom by operating on a structure that gives us choices. Through having a society built on choices, we feel as though we are experiencing freedom, but what we are truly experiencing is the opportunity to choose between a controlled series of choices. In other words, our life is built on multiple-choice questions where the answers are limited, but they still provide options, nonetheless.

The best way that you can avoid being subjected to these types of manipulative behaviors is to recognize them when they are taking place and educate yourself on the options available to you and what rights you have in your position. If you are being exposed to manipulative controlled decisions by someone or something that you can avoid, avoiding that person or place may be your best option to avoid being manipulated. However, if you are being forced to make a decision, make a decision that is going to work in your best interest, and then, if it truly means something to you, learn about how you can contribute to making the system better so that your options are more reasonable in the future.

You should also beware of anyone who is trying to pressure you into making decisions by giving you limited options, especially when these limited options do not seem favorable, and the decision is being applied with pressure. For example, say someone is trying to sell you something, and they present you with two offers. As they present you with these two offers, they begin applying a significant amount of pressure and start bombarding you with reasons one option is better than the other option. It is likely that this type of scenario features manipulation, as this person is trying to pressure you into feeling as though your only options are to purchase one or the other. By bombarding you with information and applying pressure, they are trying to encourage you to forget that saying no is also an option. Through this tactic, they can get you to purchase something from them even if you did not need it or even want it in the first place. This type of behavior is manipulative and can lead to you making unwanted decisions because you feel as though you have no control over the situation. To avoid these types of experiences, the best thing you can do for yourself is to remember that no is always an option, and empower yourself to say no when the options being presented to you are not reasonable. This way, you can avoid making an unwanted decision in the face of stress because you will remember how to take back control and make a rational decision that fits your needs or desires.

A Desire to Be Part of Something Larger than Themselves

Humans are driven by their need to be a part of a community. Our longing for love, acceptance, and company keeps us constantly searching for something to be a part of. Most of us do not feel "complete" unless we are a part of something bigger than ourselves, often in alignment with a larger group of other people. This is why many people support things like religions and cultures because these are opportunities to be a part of something that is bigger. Together, the community joins to be a part of something meaningful, often engaging in traditions as a way to keep themselves working toward something that has a purpose. Based on this particular need or behavioral law, people are drawn into various groups that are larger than themselves and that align with their core beliefs and values.

The type of power that originally set out to manipulate people based on this human nature was charlatans. Initially, charlatans would focus on building small groups around themselves and then selling them things such as magical elixirs that were promised to grant blessings such as immortality and superior health. One day, they accidentally stumbled on this law of human nature when they began seeing the groups around them grow larger and larger. As they found, the bigger the group became, the more powerful they managed to be. They would become so powerful that even when people realized that their elixirs were often bogus, their other loyal followers would defend them and protect them against the disbelievers. Any deficiencies in their ideas would be hidden by the sheer mass of their following and the devotion that their "fans" had toward them and their "abilities".

The best way to understand how charlatanism and cults work is to understand how cults are built. This is not so that you can go on to develop your own cult, but instead so that you can understand the methodology behind them so that you can avoid being drawn into one and build immunity to the manipulation tactics that they use. By having a deep understanding of the five steps used to build a cult, you can educate yourself on what these steps look like and avoid being duped by them.

Demanding Special Treatment

People adore being treated like they are special or unique in some way as this makes them feel important and nurtures their sense of ego. Often, this is not intended to be shallow or superficial. Instead, they genuinely feel good when they are being treated like they are important. Feeling important often coincides with receiving positive attention, which is something that every single human, from babies to the elderly, craves. When you receive positive attention, it boosts your self-esteem, improves your self-confidence, and leaves you feeling like you are capable of achieving anything that you desire in life. When someone loves you unconditionally, shows you an immense amount of support, or treats you like your talents are something especially unique, it feels good. You start to take pride in what you are doing, and you may even do a little more so that you can show off even more of your talents and receive an even greater amount of positive attention or praise from the people who are stimulating these feelings in you.

This is not only done in abusive relationships between lovers, relatives, or friends either. This type of behavior happens regularly from manipulative people all the time. In many cases, manipulative leaders will use this type of behavior to manipulate their entire audience into feeling important so that they can manipulate their audience into becoming dependent on them and the attention they provide. The same can happen in sales or among corporate individuals. People will try to win you over by making you feel important and smart, and then, once they have, they manipulate you into giving them what they want and then completely abandon you once you do.

Among manipulative leaders, some of the most common manipulative power plays that play on people's desire to feel special include dumbing themselves down, using selective honesty, and playing the courtier to others. Through these three actions, they can "butter people up" so that they are vulnerable to their other manipulative behaviors, thus leaving the manipulator in the perfect position to get whatever they want. If you want to avoid being manipulated by having someone stroke your ego while they stab you in the back, you need to be on the lookout for these behaviors and practice protecting yourself any time you see them being enacted.

Chapter 9: Strategies of Dark Psychology

Some psychologists believe that everyone has the capability of accessing the dark side of their personality, the side that operates without a moral or ethical standard and makes decisions not on reason but on personal satisfaction and gain, or pleasure among other less than noble reasons. The majority of people control these tendencies; others choose to act.

Dark psychology is the science of manipulation and mind control, especially as it applies to people who use tactics of persuasion, mind control, manipulation, and coercion for the benefit of themselves. It is the study of those who prey upon others, usually in a malevolent or sometimes criminal way.

When these manifest, especially in those for whom their dark side is their usual side, traits such as callousness, being highly manipulative, impulsivity, and grandiosity are common among those who operate in the fringe. For these individuals, persuasion is a means to their ends, and unsuspecting people are caught in their traps.

Several infamous individuals come to mind when discussing dark psychology.

Charles Manson is one of those who used the concepts of manipulation to orchestrate murder. He is considered a psychopath. These individuals are often considered charming and friendly, and they possess charisma. They are also impulsive and selfish, have a lack of empathy, and have no remorse for their actions.

Bernie Madoff was convicted of a scheme to con people out of money. In dark psychology, he would be categorized as Machiavellian—named after Niccolò Machiavelli, an Italian Renaissance diplomat and writer born in 1469. He is accused of influencing the French Government's crackdowns and attacks against the Huguenots in France. A person or organization that bears the label of Machiavellian is skilled at using manipulation for deceptive and exploitive gains.

Many entertainments and sports superstars are narcissistic in nature, another of the dark personality traits. Narcissists have inflated opinions about themselves, are considered braggarts, and demand attention. Think of those people who need to be the center of attention, those who may be considered divas, and those who let everyone know how special they are.

Machiavellianism, psychopathy, and narcissism are often referred to as the dark triad, a term that is used as a forewarning indication of criminal behavior as well as a problematic relationship with others.

However, the tactics used in dark psychology are not only reserved for the criminal element in society. These manipulation methods are also used to sell products and services, to seek election, or achieve social status, and even by family members to get what they want. People who want to feel superior to others, those who take advantage of others, those who value winning above everything else, and those who prey on people's emotions are examples of how dark psychology manifests in everyday life.

A book that was written by Robert Greene, *The 48 Laws of Power*, serves as a sort of technical manual on the manipulation techniques used in dark psychology. He identified ways people can manipulate others to gain power. These ways are unsettling because these operate outside of a moral compass. Nevertheless, these tactics are used by people and organizations to control and persuade.

The first of these is to "never outshine the master." Making those in charge feel they are superior is a way to manipulate the situation to a person's benefit. It strokes the ego of those who are in a position of authority and complimenting someone is a way of getting their attention.

Another of Greene's laws is not to put too much trust in friends, especially in the workplace, and learn to use your enemies. Friends will not be as loyal as an enemy who has much to prove, according to Greene. He advises considering who best can serve your interests in helping you achieve your goals and not to let loyalty or friendship cloud that decision.

To manipulate and gain power over others, an influencer should confuse, misdirect, and keep information known to him or her close at hand. The idea is to make sure people don't know for certain what you know or what you can do. Once your aspirations are revealed, a person loses power over others. Their cover is blown. Along with this is the advice to say less than necessary. Don't give others the information that you need to achieve your goals. Always practice the art of deception.

Another way that dark psychology is used is that influencers will protect their reputation but seek ways to used others' transgressions against them. Anticipating potential attacks against your credibility is first and foremost the way to guard your reputation, and thus your standing in the eyes of others. Be scrupulous in bringing out enemies' missteps and let their reputations be dismantled by public opinion.

When you do go after a rival or an enemy, make sure you deliver fatal blows to their reputation and status. Keep the pressure on them to erode their confidence, spirit, health, and wellbeing. Someone who is fully devastated will have less opportunity to challenge you in the future.

Attention should always focus on yourself. Don't lose yourself in the crowd. Don't blend in. Grab the spotlight, but don't reveal too much about yourself at once. Know when to make your presence in a person's life, group, or organization scarce. The saying "Absence makes the heart grow fonder" is appropriate for this dark psychology tactic. Make sure your presence in the group or love interest's life is secure, and then drop off the *radar* for a while. You will again be the center of interest and the focus of discussion. Just as scarcity can raise the value and desire for an item, the same can be accomplished for you.

People will gravitate toward the person who gets attention, which raises your prestige. Make people come to you for advice, help, information, or any other reason that makes you the authority. By forcing others to act or enticing your enemies to seek you out, you have the control. Put people in an unfamiliar territory to exert your influence over them.

Use other people to accomplish the work you have been tasked with completing and then take the credit for a job well done. By doing this, you achieve recognition without having to do the work. Don't make an appeal for mercy in getting others to do your work. Always appeal to their self-interests.

Give the other choices, but make sure those choices are the ones you want them to make.

For example, they have a choice in giving you more authority or trying to accomplish their goals without you. Make sure you hold power no matter the situation but make them feel like they had a choice if they hesitate, up the terms of the deal. Each day lost means more money to pay or concessions being made to you.

If you make a mistake, don't admit it. Blame someone else for it. Avoid reproach, hide your error, and don't appear to let a mistake bother you.

Keep people depending on you, make your presence in their lives invaluable, and be the reason for their happiness. This ensures your independence and freedom to do as you want.

Keep focused on your interests and goals and refuse pressure to commit to a person or cause. By maintaining your independence, people will chase you and manipulate others to seek your commitment to them. Play hard to get to increase respect.

Don't let anyone in on the tricks you use to achieve success. Make it appear as if your success is a walk in the park like it is easily accomplished with no major challenges. It should seem natural and appear that there is no hard work involved in these successes.

Avoid unhappy people or those who are unlucky. Don't let others' emotions cloud your judgment. Stay disconnected from anyone who cannot contribute to your power status. Do not close yourself off completely from those who may threaten your position in power. It is better to be out in the open and gather information than be vulnerable to the unknown.

Generate a group of people to believe in you by utilizing the characteristics of cults. Be vague about who you are, but give them something to believe in. Use vagueness in words and actions, but generate emotions tied to people's desire to believe and have faith. Go with excitement and encouragement instead of rationalizations. Have rituals and require sacrifice. Play up the "us versus them" scenarios.

Bring people into your power by breaking them down. Work on their personality traits, fears, and weaknesses to bring them into your control. Use gentleness to avoid their resentment and hatred but continue to chip away until they become a supporter and are willing to do what you ask them to do.

Present yourself in the way in which you want to be treated, much like royalty does when entering a room or a keynote speaker does when they are called to the conference stage. Make yourself stand out in a positive way. Act confident, respect yourself and create the illusion of your greatness. Admit small flaws. Don't appear to be perfect. Share thoughts and defects to be regarded as approachable.

Play to each person's perception of themselves. Help them find someone or something to blame. Mining the victim's fantasies increases your power over them and your ability to control what they do and say.

Find their weakness and exploit it. Insecurity, emotions that are out of control, or a vice that is kept secret are common ones. Pay attention to what they say, how they act in various situations, and the things they share with you. Delve into their past to hone in on the signs that can point to these weaknesses. If they cannot control their emotions, use this to your advantage. If they indulge in vices or guilty pleasures, find ways to expose their vulnerabilities.

Use honesty selectively and as a means to disarm others of their perceptions of you. An occasional kind act overwhelms any unkind acts you may have previously committed. It takes people off balance and makes them question their opinion of you. When their guard is down, you can then present yourself as a friend, but use them to gain information or power.

Be unpredictable when it is in your benefit to do so. You don't want others to recognize behavior patterns. This protects your control and power. Keeping people guessing and struggling for an explanation weakens them and makes them more susceptible to your suggestions and demands.

Create the persona you want to be. Don't let others' opinions of you determine what your role should be. Claim your power and strive to perfect this persona. Remember to regard your actions and how you present yourself as part of the overall scheme, much like an actor playing a role. Embrace and incorporate the power aspects into your social skills and interpersonal dealings.

If you can't win, surrender. The decision to stand down is an unsettling one for your opponent. Human nature calls for meeting an act of aggression with an act of aggression. Choosing to surrender or move on buys you time to retaliate later, and with much greater force.

Imitation may be a form of flattery, but to a person who is seeking control or power, it is infuriating. Use this tactic to unhinge your enemies into overreacting. It can also convince them that you share the same values, which lets their guard down and opens the door for your manipulation attempts.

Use tactics to stir up trouble without pulling yourself into the quagmire. Don't show anger or emotion but rile these up in your enemies. Let their emotions take over to reflect badly on themselves.

When you take action, do so boldly. Make others believe you are confident in your decision and don't hesitate once you have engaged in the action or the lie. Let your boldness continue to misdirect. Note that a bigger target yields a higher reward for you.

Become skilled in choosing your victims. Not everyone will react the same way. Learn their patterns of behavior and modify your approaches. Take care not to offend the wrong person, the one who can help you gain the power you crave. Inflate the ego of your victim to hide your intentions and disarm their self-protection mechanisms.

Don't fall for others' attempts to persuade you with gifts or favors. Don't accept gifts to avoid the need to express gratitude. Be generous to gain power and benefit from others' feelings of gratitude and obligation.

Patience may be a virtue, but it is also a tool in planning your actions. Take time to establish yourself in the game, wait for the right time to take action, and patiently gather information to give you an edge.

Introduce change slowly. Always make it seem like an improvement or that it benefits others in some way. Indicate that you respect the traditional ways, and introduce changes a little at a time.

Target those who may be influencing others in opposition to your goals. Get rid of the opposition, and those who are in that camp will have nowhere to go. Identify the troublemakers—that is, those who are unhappy, dissatisfied, or ill at ease. Don't let their discontent affect the others. Make others aware of who the problem is and let others rid the group of the problem.

Learn to play the game. Flatter sparingly to make it seem sincere. Change your message and language based on the person you are dealing with at that moment. Seek out the limelight. Don't share negative information. Be nonchalant about the business at hand. Don't court favors from your boss. Keep your emotions under control, and act with restraint in group settings.

Under all circumstances, don't share your thoughts about your goals or your plans to achieve them. Play for the crowd. Reinforce their opinions and blend in when needed. Don't let people think you need their attention or that you are superior to them. Think about it, but don't give it away.

If something is outside of your reach or influence, ignore it. If something causes you irritation, ignore it. If someone tries to usurp your authority, ignore them. When you ignore something or someone, it trivializes their importance. People don't protect what is trivial, thus opening the door to you getting what you want.

Make every action impressive. The more extravagant, the better; the more sensational, the more power it brings. Make sure that what you showcase awes those around you and increases your standing in that circle.

Make sure you keep planning your scheme to the very end, and that is when you win. Use long-range planning to keep the goal in mind and create the scenarios that will move you closer to that finale.

Remember to be strategic and plan every move. Planning builds confidence and keeps you from being taken by surprise. Consider the "what ifs" and adjust accordingly.

Plan an original course, not one that someone else has tried. It's hard to gain respect when you simply repeat. Find your own path, and turn the focus onto you and not a predecessor.

Keep the plan to yourself. Don't divulge your goals or the motives you are using to get to the end. Be adaptable and change direction when needed. Keep moving toward the goal in unpredictable ways.

When you reach the goal you set, be ready to stop. Continuing to press on can create dissatisfaction and disillusionment. Accept the win.

Many of these power laws have likely been used in some measure by everyone. You may even have recognized yourself or someone you know as these were explained.

Have you ever given someone a compliment, purchased a small gift or done a special task to get them to agree to a request? That's identified as love flooding. Have you ever told an untruth, a little white lie, or even a whopper of a lie to get out of trouble? Have you ever given someone you care about the cold shoulder as a punishment for something they said or did? That's called love denial. How about giving someone the silent treatment? That's withdrawal. Have you ever offered choices to someone, but only presented the ones that are best for you? That's a choice restriction. Have you ever used reverse psychology?

All these are common ways to influence other people using elements of dark psychology.

While many of the power-grabbing tactics identified by Greene come about through routine interactions in a social or business setting, the online world is also a battleground. Cybercriminals use these tactics to get what they want—access to personal information to commit identity fraud or to steal money and affection from vulnerable and lonely people. Cyberterrorists and those with political agendas also gain when they use these methodologies to gain control, exploit, stalk, and manipulate victims.

Understanding the ways people gain power and acceptance puts you in control when dark psychology is being used against you or to keep you from utilizing these techniques against others. To protect yourself and keep your persuasion efforts from crossing the line, assess the situation and the person and determine what the benefit will be and what your goal is in this situation. Determine whether the tactics you are using make you feel good, honest, and guilt-free. The question of whether there will be benefits in the long term as a result of this interaction determine if there are other ways to achieve the result you need without compromising your ethics.

Chapter 10: Manipulation and Neuro-linguistic Programming

What Is Neuro-linguistic Programming?

Neuro-linguistic programming, or NLP, in simplest terms, is the programming language of your mind. We've all had instances where we attempted to communicate with someone who doesn't speak our language. The outcome? They didn't understand us!

You go to a restaurant abroad and ask for a fancy steak but end up receiving insipid stew owing to the misinterpretation of language and codes.

This is what happens when we try to communicate with our subconscious mind. We think we are commanding it to give us happier relationships, more money, a better job, and other, similar things. However, if that's not what is showing up, something is being lost in translation. The subconscious/unconscious mind has the power to help us accomplish our goals only if we program it using codes it recognizes and understands.

If you are asking your unconscious mind for steak and receiving stew, it is time to speak its language. Think of NLP as a user manual for the brain. When people master NLP, they become fluent in the language of the subconscious mind, which is excellent when it comes to reprogramming their own and other people's thoughts, ideas and beliefs. This gives them the power to influence and persuade people and, on the downside, even manipulate them.

Neuro-linguistic programming is a set of techniques, methods, and tools for enhancing communication with deeper layers of our brain. It is an approach that combines personal development, psychotherapy, and communication. Its creators (John Grinder and Richard Bandler) claim that there is a strong link between language, behavior patterns, and neurological processes, which can be used for enhancing learning and personal development.

Influence versus Manipulation

So do you believe a hammer is a tool of utility or destruction? Well, it depends on how you use it, right? Or what purpose you use it for.

NLP is potent when it comes to getting people to do what you want them to. It is the hammer that can be used to fix a nail in the wall or destroy a piece of wood. Similarly, NLP can be used to build something positive, or it can be used for a destructive purpose (manipulation).

NLP and manipulation have nearly the same meaning. Both are about generating the desired effect on other people without obvious exertion. However, one key difference between influence and manipulation is that the latter is meant to influence others to meet the manipulator's selfish goals through means that can be unfair, unlawful, sneaky, or insidious. Things are contrived through underhanded methods to turn out in favor of the manipulator. A manipulator often preys on the insecurities, fears, and guilt of other people. In turn, victims of manipulation feel dissatisfied, frustrated, trapped, and unhappy.

Conversely, influence is the ability to inspire people in an admirable, charismatic, and honorable way. We are often inspired by influential people and aspire to model our life on theirs. There is a general feeling of positivity related to them, and we feel positively impacted in their company. Not every influence is positive, which is why we use terms such as "bad influence" to signify a person's negative effect on us. However, manipulation is never categorized as good or bad. It always operates with sinister motives. That is the primary difference between influence and manipulation.

Influence is a double-edged sword that can be used positively and negatively, while manipulation only operates with a negative, narrow, and selfish perspective to meet the objectives of the manipulator.

While manipulation has self-centered and questionable motives, influence can also be positive. In contrast to manipulation, influence has positive connotations, which considers other people's needs, goals, and desires. Don't we, as parents, want to influence our children to lead happier and healthier lives? Similarly, as a manager, we want to influence our team to put in their best efforts.

Just like the hammer discussed above, people can use NLP for positively or negatively influencing people to meet their selfish objectives (manipulation). NLP is a mind-control tool that can do both—build and damage.

NLP Strategies

A strategy in NLP is a combination of representations, both internal and external, that produces the same specific result consistently. It is a series of steps that we program our mind and body automatically to do to achieve a planned outcome.

Have you ever wondered how one person could see something one way and another person can see the same situation or event and view it completely differently? Have you ever wondered how they could think that way about something that, to you, is so patently black and white?

Would you like to know how to tap into people's thought processes? Would it serve you beneficially if you knew what another person's hot buttons are and what it is that makes someone tick? Would you like to know what it is that motivates others to take action?

Well, that is precisely what the strategies of NLP enable you to do. It is a form of mind control, brainwashing, or self-hypnosis, for the lack of better analogies. However, what NLP truly is about is the way we communicate—the way we communicate with ourselves, internally and externally, and communicate more effectively with others.

We perform these strategies every day, mostly unconsciously, because we have programmed our mind how to think about certain things. Taking a shower or driving to work are good examples of how we allow our subconscious brain to wash and drive to work. We rarely give these routine acts much thought; we just allow our mind to react with certain behaviors to produce the actions required to reach an end.

So since we already have proven that these strategies work and that we already are using them to control certain aspects of our lives, can we train our brains to react at a subconscious level for others things too? Of course, we can.

We develop our life patterns as strategies for doing things since birth when we discovered that if we cry, our need for food and a clean diaper are met. We discovered a way to achieve certain ends and accomplished what it is that we needed. We discovered what has worked and have internalized the process that we have used successfully in the past to influence ourselves into making it work.

We use these subconscious strategies in everything that we do in life. So in short, an NLP strategy is something that we have done over and over in our mind, and we have developed a process for achievement.

Now just remember, NLP teaches us to deal with form as opposed to content. It is not about what you thought about; it is how you thought about it. Did you create a picture of it in your mind's eye? Were there certain words that you used to think about it? Do you hear a voice in your head about it? Was it your voice or someone else's? How did it make you feel? Did you experience any emotions about it? NLP teaches us strategies on context, process, and form instead of focusing on the content of something.

Modeling

Modeling is a strategy developed in NLP to tap into someone's belief systems by observing their physiology and intellectual strategies. We do this by discovering what another person's mental program is, or mental syntax. The internal syntax of a person is a vital element in modeling. Once we learn their internal syntax, we learn what strategy they use in the decision-making process.

Say you have a Russian male friend who comes by at times and who speaks very little English, but you have formed a bond of communication that allows you to speak together. The first thing that you do is study how he communicates—what little English words he uses and how he uses them. You notice a pattern of speech that includes inflection (it's not what you say, it's how you say it) and what terminology he uses to determine if he is a visual, auditory, or kinesthetic person. This is how you will pattern your speech to him for a better understanding.

Then you would model his syntax by putting certain words in a certain order. A well-used example here would be the difference in meaning in the phrases "The dog bit Johnny" and "Johnny bit the dog"—same words but just arranged in a different order to produce a completely different meaning, especially if you were Johnny or the dog. The different interpretation is caused by the sequential arrangement of the words. We would also mimic body language and facial expressions. We may even develop our interpretation of a Russian accent—all in the effort to communicate effectively.

Now, this is a strategy that we have developed that can be taken and relocated, enabling us to change the context of how we perceive something to be and change it. We cannot change the content, but we can surely change the context by using the mental strategies that NLP has taught us.

You cannot change the thing that causes a certain reaction. For example, you cannot turn an apple into a lemon, no matter how hard you try. However, you most certainly can elicit a response that makes you think of the lemon more than the apple. This is focusing completely on how someone processes information and will enable you to install it in someone else, simply by knowing the strategy they use to process information and how to change another person's strategy.

This is an ever-evolving process that people can use to learn, change, and achieve any goal that we set. We have all the answers within ourselves to solve any problem that we perceive. We have all the resources of the universe at our disposal for success. We just need to exercise our decision-making muscles and develop a cognitive strategy.

The TOTE Method

One of the foundational strategies of NLP is called TOTE and was adapted by NLP cofounders Bandler and Grinder, from a book by George Miller, and it is a strategy designed to teach us how people process and retain information. The acronym TOTE stands for test, operate, test again, and exit.

Test

The gathering of information processed sets up the trigger and is the beginning of this strategy. This leads us to the second step: operate.

This is where you take action from the results of the first test, measuring where it stands compared to the result desired. Then it goes to the third step which is another modified test. This pattern is repeated until it reaches an acceptable level of outcome. It is at this point of acceptance that you *exit*. An exit can also be made when it becomes evident that the desired outcome cannot be met.

It is the first step that establishes an outcome by testing conditions that begin the strategy. For example, what is it that makes you feel motivated? What is the trigger that gets you out of bed in the morning? There is usually something like family, bills, planning a vacation—anything that gets you personally motivated. Is it something you feel, see, or hear? Think back on a time when you felt the most motivated. What buttons did it push for you? What triggered these feelings of motivation? It is vital that you relive this moment in the process of creating new strategies that you develop a specific pattern for and know exactly what triggered you to feel the most motivated you have ever felt. You must find a specific trigger that has set you off in the past that can be duplicated easily and subconsciously.

Operation

Access and gather data necessary that pertains to the strategy you are developing. The first batch of data that you need to access is VAK (visual, auditory, kinesthetic) external. The goal here is to make it internal by either remembering or creating new data—memories or data that you construct yourself. So the operation consists of three types of external data and two types of internal data.

Test Again

The third phase (*test-operate-test*) is a testing stage that measures comparison and gauge progress. Progress is used to determine when the strategy is complete. It is a comparison between the new data against the old. If it matches the desired outcome, you can move to Exit.

Exit

The exit is when you have developed a new representation, and your mission has been accomplished. There may be a loop of *test-operate-test* until this strategy can be considered complete. As pointed earlier, the first test is the trigger, used to acquire and process information. The trigger is used to propel you toward the second test, which compares the information gathered through the operations phase of accessing and creating data. Once the second test is achieved, the strategy is successful and complete where you can then exit.

This is the subconscious process of sequences of external and internal representations that control your behavior. Once a specific neuro pattern occurs, then the appropriate behavior is generated.

The Strategy of Elicitation

There are formal and informal types of elicitation strategies. The modalities of each user must be discovered to determine how they process information. Informal elicitations are those which come naturally during a conversation, while formal elicitations may require some digging; however, people behave internally and react in kind as to what they are talking about. They demonstrate, verbally and nonverbally, the strategies they use every day to process information by accessing those emotions.

Formal Elicitation

The following is a sample of how a formal elicitation can be used. You are advised to go over this information until you fully understand how it works and how you can inject it into your communications with others.

Informal Elicitation

Once you have mastered the strategy of formal elicitation, you should easily master informal elicitation. You can literally understand what makes a person tick by simply asking and effectively listening to how they respond to simple inquiries. An example would be, "Nice shoes, what made you decide to buy them?" Listen to how they respond. Look at their eye movements and any nonverbal responses. Successful salespeople do this all the time. A prospect will tell you exactly how they should be sold to, and all you would have to do is listen and observe. They will tell you how and why they do whatever it is that they do.

Eye Patterns

Eye patterns are a good nonverbal indicator and informal elicitation. Ask someone, as we did above, as to "what made them decide to buy those shoes." Subconsciously they will move their eyes in certain directions as they recall what they thought when they purchased their shoes. This is how people process information, essentially reliving the event in their head. The way to develop the sensory acuity necessary to read eye patterns effectively is to (as always) practice, practice, and practice. Be well grounded and know how to read eye patterns very well. This way, eventually the information will just come to you without thought as your subconscious takes over and makes this strategy a part of your normal behavior.

Study eye patterns and make written notes for future study. As with any elicitation exercise, TOTE tests them until they are precise. The NLP eye strategies are extremely powerful once mastered.

It is also possible to use a person's natural eye patterns as a means of changing how they feel about a past experience, and thus about aspects of their life that relate to that experience. These steps include the following:

Planning. This step is relatively standard and includes an evaluation and a detailed history of the issue in question. This step is very interested in the subject's past, specifically distressing memories which are then tagged as targets of reprocessing. The goal is to typically focus on the biggest and most difficult experiences the subject has been through as changing those will then cause the most noticeable change overall.

Learn to relax. An important part of the process is staying calm between sessions prior to learning to direct your eye movements yourself. Because of this, therapists suggest and help practice various relaxation techniques, including guided imagery prior to getting into actual eye movement techniques. Another particularly useful relaxation technique that can aid in this step is mindfulness meditation.

Being mindful is a process of existing completely in the moment, using the information your senses are providing you as an anchor to prevent you from interacting with the thoughts that are racing through your head. The goal is to notice thoughts without interacting with them, and it can make avoiding negative thoughts—before they lead to panic and anxiety—easier than you may have ever thought possible. It can be practiced anywhere at any time—all you have to do is focus on breathing deeply and the physical sensations that doing so creates throughout your body.

The nature of the added stimulus isn't important; what is important is that it remains in play long enough for the eye movement to be moved away from the trouble spot. During each session, the patient's eyes will be moved further and further from the trouble spot, improving their reaction to it in the process.

VOC scale. The VOC scale, otherwise known as the validity of the cognition scale, is what is used to calibrate a person who is going to be using this process for the first time. Initially, the patient will be asked to think of a specific image they can relate negatively to before then doing the same thing with a positive image instead. The patient will then be asked to consider how completely they believe in the positive image, followed by the negative image. They will then be asked to list any feelings that the images might generate as well as their overall level of intensity. They will finally be asked to link those sensations with various parts of the body, if relevant.

Reprocessing. The reprocessing step focuses on retraining the brain to experience positive emotions as opposed to the negative ones that are currently associated with specific memories. As a part of this exercise, the patient will focus on trouble spots for about a minute at a time. While doing so, they will also be asked to focus on something that will cause them to look either left or right, as opposed to in the way that is currently associated with the negative memory in question.

Improve beliefs. Once reprocessing has occurred a few times, the next step will be for the patient to retain the new patterns by relating back to the positive thoughts they generated earlier. This process will also include another round of the stimulus from the previous step to ensure that future negative memories generate the same mitigated response. During this step, it is crucial that the patient focuses on each part of the new emotion, including how it makes them feel both mentally and physically. After they have a strong grasp on the emotion, they will then be instructed to think about it in conjunction with the stimuli in question with enough conviction that the two become interconnected in your mind.

Seek out lingering negative sensations. Once the primary thoughts toward the trouble spots have been dealt with, the therapist will be free to move on to any lingering physical issues the trouble spots might be causing. This can manifest itself as tightness, tension, or any other out-of-place sensation that is only caused by automatic physical responses to trained mental stimuli. Steps four and five are then repeated with the physical sensation instead of the mental ones in mind.

Take care not to move past this step too quickly as it can take time for the prolonged physical effects of otherwise altered emotional responses to become apparent. It is important to stretch and exercise regularly so that you can then more easily determine any leftover stiffness or sore spots that are persisting longer than they should.

Keep a log. After the majority of the issue has been dealt with it is important to keep a log between sessions detailing any issues relating to your trouble spots that pop up during your day-to-day life. It is important that the process is applied to every tendril of thought or action that is related to the trouble spot. Only by completely retraining your mind automatically to act differently in response to stimuli will this strategy be effective. Many people find that keeping a physical log of their experiences rather than a digital one makes the issues appear more real and, as such, easier to overcome. The essential thing is that you find a recording system that works for you and get in the habit of writing in it daily.

Reassess. In response to the log you keep, your therapist will be able to determine when a specific trouble spot has been vanquished. Remember: it will be important to get into a positive routine and keep at it for as long as it takes for the negative behavior to disappear completely. The human mind likes repetition—make your life easier and form positive routines which will more easily turn into habits.

Self-Hypnosis

A note on self-hypnosis audio recordings: When you first begin using hypnotherapy, it is important to conduct sessions for at least twenty minutes at a time. Ideally, two sessions per day should be the goal as the extra repetition will help the autosuggestions enter your subconscious more efficiently. After you have been using self-hypnosis for long enough that your subconscious has become accustomed to accepting autosuggestions, you can generally reduce your sessions without losing efficacy.

While you are first starting self-hypnosis, it is important to direct the hypnosis at yourself by speaking at yourself. Start by saying you will do this or you will do that. After your mind has become accustomed to the exercise, you can switch to saying I if you prefer. With that in mind, here are some additional tips to maximize the effectiveness of each self-hypnosis session:

- Find a routine and stick with it: Your mind is programmed to enjoy routine. Take advantage of this and ensure you practice self-hypnosis at the same time every day.

- Don't lie on your back during sessions: You need to provide your full focus to what you are listening to, not spend the time fighting off sleep.

- Have different recordings for morning and evening: Include energetic suggestions in the morning and relaxing suggestions to help you sleep at night.

- Don't worry about following along: You do not consciously have to hear what you are saying on the recording. In fact, that is rather the point. Not being able to recall what you just heard is a sign the message is making its way to your subconscious.

- Section your suggestions: Suggestions and affirmations are referred to as a section. Sections usually last above five minutes and should all be generally related to a single goal. Keep each section focused on a single task. Adding a bit of music between sections will make it easier to focus on the different specifics of each one.

- Stay motivated: The more mentally prepared you are for the task at hand the more successful you will be at it.

It is also important always to pause when indicated and to do so for no more than five but no less than three seconds.

Begin

Feel yourself relaxing where you are sitting. As you become more and more comfortable, feel yourself falling into a deeper state of relaxation. Accept this state and go deeper and deeper still. Take a few deep, slow breaths, and focus on the sensations you feel as you do so.

(Pause)

Today you will find both your body and mind in a state of extreme relaxation, and this starts as you exhale and feel all the stress and tension leaving your body as you do so.

(Pause)

Focus on a single point in front of you that is free from visual distraction. Focus on this single spot to the exclusion of all else.

(Pause)

Take another long, deep breath, and feel the life-giving air racing into your lungs.

(Pause)

Feel your body becoming more and more relaxed with each breath.

(Pause)

Your body is now extremely relaxed, but your mind remains clear and focused on the task at hand. Focus on every single word.

(Pause)

Each breath propels you deeper and deeper into a calm, quiet world.

(Pause)

Each word I speak will help you sink deeper and deeper still.

(Pause)

You are alone in the universe, and nothing can prevent you from relaxing totally and completely.

(Pause)

All your thoughts and worries are meaningless right now. This time is for relaxation; nothing else exists.

(Pause)

Your muscles tense for a moment, and as they relax, you feel all your negative emotions and thoughts from the day evaporate at the same time. You feel lighter and happier than ever before.

(Pause)

Your mind and body now feel more relaxed and refreshed, ready for what is to come.

(Pause)

Your mind is focused and ready to absorb new information.

(Pause)

You are focused on the sound of my voice and are ready to take the following suggestions to heart.

Add in hypnotic suggestions.

(Pause)

Your eyes now begin to feel heavy, and as they close, you begin to feel tired. Slowly close your eyes until there is no light left.

(Pause)

Closing your eyes lets you feel even more relaxed.

(Pause)

Picture yourself with an extra eye in the center of your head and imagine what it would be like to see through that eye.

(Pause)

Now picture yourself in a place of absolute peace and happiness, your version of paradise.

(Pause)

Visualize yourself in the middle of this amazing place.

(Pause)

Feel how comfortable you are here; how relaxed.

(Pause)

Nothing in the universe can disturb your feeling of ultimate peace and tranquility.

(Pause)

I will now begin counting down from three, as I do so inhale and exhale on each number and let each breath make you even calmer and content.

(Pause)

Three, two, one.

(Pause)

Each breath you take should be more refreshing than the one before it. Now take an especially deep breath.

(Pause)

After you listen to this recording, you will find that everything you undertake will be easier than before.

(Pause)

Your mind is sharp, alert and focused and will become more so every time you hear this recording.

(Pause)

After listening to this recording, you will know that everything you want and desire is attainable. All you must do now is reach out and grab it.

(Pause)

There's nothing you want to do that can't be done.

(Pause)

When you lie down to sleep at night, sleep will come easily and will be restorative and rejuvenating.

(Pause)

If you take a nap, you will fall asleep easily, and your cares will not bother you until you awaken refreshed and ready to face the day ahead.

(Pause)

Every day is better than the one before, and tomorrow will be better still. Everything is happening as it should, and you are always in the right place at the right time.

(Pause)

There is something new to be happy about every single day.

(Pause)

Every day provides you with a chance to improve, and you take it gladly.

(Pause)

You feel great, better than ever in fact.

(Pause)

The world is your oyster. Get ready to enjoy it.

(Pause)

Focus on this feeling of relaxed success as I count down from five.

(Pause)

When I get to one, you will awaken refreshed, rejuvenated and ready to face the tasks at hand.

(Pause)

Five, four, three, two, one.

(Pause)

You will now awake feeling rejuvenated if you are starting your day or ready for a good night's sleep if you are done for the day.

(Pause)

Relearn Optimism

You can take two different people, and while they are going to react to things in life because they have different thinking processes, you are going to notice more differences than that.

If someone is happy most of the time, it is because they have trained themselves to look at the silver lining in life. Yes, they are going to have "hole in their pocket" moments, but they are not going to focus on these moments because they know that they are going to pass eventually.

Someone who is depressed is going to be focusing on all the negativity that is in their life and will not have the ability to see the world for what it truly is. The biggest difference between these two people is how they look at the world.

There are going to be cycles in everyone's life where they are going to have everything going for them, but then there are going to be times that they feel like everything is going against them. A person who is more optimistic about life is going to see all the setbacks that occur as something that is just temporary and will pass eventually. This makes that person more resilient, and therefore, they will bounce back from whatever bad happens to them faster than someone who is depressed.

A person who is depressed is going to look at their setbacks as if they are never going to end. Each bad thing that happens seems to last forever, and it doesn't matter if it only lasts a day or two or a week; to a person that is depressed, they are going to think that a day is a month and a week is a year. It is going to make it seem as if what they are going through is never going to change but last for the rest of their life. They are not going to bounce back from the bad things in their lives nearly as fast as someone who looks for the silver lining.

When you are depressed, you have learned the pessimism that you are constantly feeling. It is not something that you are born with. It is also known as permanent pervasive, which is learned helplessness. You can avoid this learned helplessness though.

The biggest difference between an optimist and a pessimist is that an optimistic person knows how to explain themselves whenever something bad happens to them. They can talk about it, and this is what empowers them to be able to look for the silver lining in the world around them.

Someone who is a permanent pervasive is not going to be able to talk about what they are going through, and this is going to cause them to be stuck in a rut.

The first step in being able to stop this learned helplessness is to recognize the patterns that are going to put you in this situation in the first place. When you begin to see that you are constantly looking at the bad in life, then you are going to be leading yourself down the road to learned helplessness. However, you can get past this with a little bit of help thanks to NLP.

Some examples of this are to remember that all the negative events are only temporary and they are only going to be specific to the situation that you are dealing with. A negative event like going through a period in your job where you are not getting the hours that you are used to is only going to be temporary. Even if you have to find another job to make sure that you get the hours that you need, you will find it and keep making the money that you are used to.

It is unavoidable; you are going to be faced with challenges in your life. However, how you deal with the situation is going to be based on your thought process when it comes to that challenge. Everything in your life can either be good or bad depending on how you look at things.

Step one. Accept that you are going through the challenge. Most people tend to try and make the problem smaller than it is or dismiss it because they do not want to accept it as happening. However, to get past it, you have to accept that there is a challenge and that you need to overcome it.

Step two. Take action. No challenge is ever going to be fixed by sitting around doing nothing. So make a plan that is going to help you overcome this challenge so you can put it into action.

Step three. Track your challenge. Talk to people who are going to be able to help you to understand what is going on in your life. If you are having problems at work or school, talk to your boss or teacher so that you can get it worked out.

Step four. Look at all the information that you have about the situation. What resources can you use to get past this? Figuring out the resources that are going to help you best is going to be one of the best ways for you to be able to know what it is that you need to do to get past this challenge. For example, if you are having trouble grasping a concept, then you should go to a coworker and see if they know how to explain it differently so that you can understand it.

Step five. Not sure what else you can do? Research! The internet is full of people that have gone through similar situations as you and they are going to have the appropriate information needed for you to get past this. Not just that, but you are going to find books that will help you out as well if that is the route that you feel like going down. This is a good way to help you not feel like you are the only person in the world going through this.

Step six. Look at all the possibilities of all the choices that you have. Each choice is going to lead to a different result, and you need to know what some of the outcomes are going to be based on what choice you make.

Step seven. The chances are that what you are going through is not only going to include you. You need to talk to the other people who are involved in the situation so that you are making sure to make the choice that is not going to harm anyone. Harming someone else is just going to bring a whole new challenge that you are going to have to deal with.

Step eight. Sometimes you are going to need a mentor to help you get through your challenge. Find someone whom you can talk to or get advice from. This does not have to be an actual person; it can be a website or even a book. However, if you are talking to someone, make sure that you can trust them with what you are saying and know that they are truly going to be there to help you instead of just saying stuff that is not going to do you any good.

Step nine. Keep on trying. You are going to end up making the wrong choice, but hopefully, you can go back and make the proper decision. Keep trying different solutions until you find the one that is right for you.

Chapter 11: Understanding Deception

Deception is another key aspect that comes with dark psychology. Like many other tactics that come with dark psychology, it is sometimes difficult to tell whether one instance of deception is considered dark or not. But before we explore this more, we first need to understand what deception is all about in our world.

Deception is going to be any word or action that is capable of making someone believe something that is not true. Fraudulently providing evidence for something that is false, implying falsehood, omitting the truth, and lying are all examples of deception.

Not all types of deception will count as dark psychology. Everyone is going to deceive others to some extent or another they may deceive others because they feel inadequate, embarrassed, or even as a kindness. For example, some studies have shown that many men lie about their height. This doesn't mean that they practice dark psychology. Also, it is common for people to deceive themselves about a range of issues such as their happiness, ambition, and health.

Deception is going to become dark any time when it is carried out with an indifferent or negative intention toward the victim. Dark deception is an understanding that the truth is not going to serve the deceptive aims of the deceiver. The deceiver is going to take the truth and either ignore, hide, or change it in favor of a version of events that suits their purpose a little bit better. Those who employ dark deception mean to do it as a way to harm rather than to help. They want to help out their interests, but they don't care who gets hurt in the process.

The Deception Spectrum

Deception can happen either on a small or large scale. Many people assume that deception has to occur on a large scale to be important. However, dark deception is present in all parts of the spectrum, and it is essential to be on the lookout at all times to ensure that you are safe.

Dark deceivers will often use the smaller deceptions to help them out as well. They may start out with some of these small deceptions to test out the victim and to condition that victim to believe the larger lies the deceiver uses later on.

Smaller deceptions can also be carried out with the goal of undermining the trust the victim has in their powers of reason and logic. If the manipulator can deceive the victim over a smaller issue, and the victim starts to question what is happening, the victim may conclude that their suspicion is irrational, and they cannot trust their judgment. Most people will start to conclude that it is their judgment that is at fault here, rather than entertaining the idea that someone else is deceiving them over some issue that seems so small. Of course, the dark deceiver is aware of this trust that people generally have, and they will try to exploit it.

A dark deceiver can also work with a large-scale deception as well. One of the largest deceptions that they can use is to convince someone that you are someone else. Not in terms of just a personality trait or some other small detail. A true deceiver can even hide their entire identity. They will hide their date of birth, name, and everything else. This is done to help push forward the goals or the agenda of the manipulator.

Deceptive Topics

Everyone has heard the saying "Money is the root of all evil." This may seem like an exaggeration, but money can often be the root of a variety of deceptions. Deception and money more often than not cross paths. Some people are going to deceive in the hopes of attaining money; others will do it to hide their money, and so much more. Because money shows up as a topic so often when it comes to deception, we are going to take a look at it now.

Take a look at a professional beggar. These individuals are going to try to get money from the public, even though they have plenty of their own. These beggars are going to use a few different dark psychological principles to get the money they want from their innocent victims. Such beggars are even willing to put some injuries on their bodies to look more desperate.

Personal marital status is another area where people are going to deceive. Sometimes, a person may try to hide their married background in the hopes of seducing a new victim. This could be for sexual or financial reasons. There are even other people who have multiple wives that are spread out across the world—wives who have no idea about one another. This deception type has become even harder with the beginning of the internet and the ability to check in on people through social media. These deceivers can manage more than one wife from each other through many different means.

Some people may appear to be falsely married when they are not. A married couple is one that is often seen as more trustworthy compared to one that is not married. The dark manipulator is aware of this idea and may choose to use it for their end goals. Some people may try to have a pretend marriage to help with taxes and insurance. One of the most common deception types with this is when the deceiver creates a fictional dead wife or husband to gain the sympathy of those around them and often their money.

A deceiver may also try to hide their criminal background. This is because it is hard to be trusted, either personally or professionally, if you have committed certain crimes. Many manipulators feel like they can use deception to hide any socially unacceptable or abnormal feelings that they have. This can stop the victim from being alerted to the person they are dealing with until it is way too late.

For example, a dark manipulator may decide that they only want to use their victim for sex. But they know that if they focus on this topic, it is going to be a red flag and hard for them to get what they want. They then decide to deceive the victim. They may overtly lie and then imply that their true intention here is commitment and love. The victim is going to fall for this deception, the exploitation from that manipulator is done, and then the victim is the one harmed by the deception.

In a romantic relationship, the manipulator is often going to hide their true intentions. Deceptive actions and words are going to leave the victim feeling that the other person is exactly what they were looking for at that moment in time. The reason that this happens is that the manipulator can identify someone who is vulnerable and then probe into their needs and weak points. The manipulator is then able to use this information and cloaks themselves, so they appear to be something they aren't. This is a common beginning with the manipulator that can turn into more long-term manipulations that the victim isn't aware of.

Deceptive Tactics

There are many different deceptive tactics that the manipulator can use at their disposal. Remember that this deception is the process of hiding information from the victim to reach their overall goals.

There are four categories of tactics that fall into deception, and any given deception is likely to involve a blend of each of them, which can make it even harder for the victim to figure out what is going on.

The first deceptive tactic that can be used is lying. This is the first technique that the manipulator is going to choose as soon as they know that the victim is susceptible to lies and has trouble figuring out the truth. This is often because the victim is someone who trusts others. Or the manipulator may have worked on this victim for some time so that they lower their guard. The manipulator is also able to find ways to hide up the lies and then explain the discrepancies if the victim starts to notice.

Any deception that occurs with lying is likely to occur in a way that is very subtle and is thought out ahead of time. A deceiver is going to embed their lie into some truthful information. For example, the manipulator would start out with a story that is about ninety percent true and ten percent false. Because it sounds legitimate and most of the story can be proven as true, the victim will think the whole story is true.

Implying is another form of deception. Implying is when the manipulator is going to suggest something false is true rather than boldly stating it. If the manipulator wants to deceive a victim about how much money they have, then they could either lie or imply. A lie would be something like, "Oh, I'm a successful guy. I've made a lot of money," even though the manipulator knows this information is not true. However, when they imply they are rich, they may say something like, "It's so stressful trying to handle things with my accountant. Trying to get my tax bill down takes up a lot of my time." The manipulator has acted and spoken in a way that makes the other person think they are wealthy, but they never state it.

Omission is another option for the deceiver. This is a failure to mention something, usually a fact that is pretty important, that is true. Omission doesn't use falsehood to cover the truth like the other two options. Instead, this one is going to ignore the truth or just leave it out. Often this piece of information is important for the victim to know about to make an informed decision. The manipulator would leave this out to protect themselves and ensure that the victim didn't have all the information.

One way that the deceiver can use omission is to create their own emotional fence with that situation. This is a tactic where the manipulator implies that a particular period of their life, or some specific topic, is painful or uncomfortable for them to discuss. The victim, feeling bad and wanting to be considerate, will avoid bringing up this topic. This gives the manipulator a chance to avoid the truth while still making the victim feel guilty when they try to bring up that painful topic.

And the final form of deception is going to be the most elaborate, and often criminal, form. This is known as fraud. Instead of the deceiver simply lying about something from the past, this kind of deceit is going to have false stories, documents, and some other evidence to back up whatever their lie says. The deceiver is going to use these things subtly. They would never say something like "I'm a doctor, take a look at my certificate!"

Instead, they will use some subtle displays to show off to the victim. They will try to steer away from being too pushy with their fraudulent claims because they know that doing this will make the victim feel that something is wrong with the situation.

Fraud is becoming more common than ever because of the internet. Deceivers can often work with some professional software to make documents that look pretty realistic, no matter what type of document they need. This can make it really hard to tell whether you are working with someone who is telling you the truth or deceiving you.

When this dark deception starts to enter the realm of fraudulence, it can be a bad sign. It shows that the deceiver is dangerous and committed to sticking with that dark psychology. They are risking serious criminal charges to do this kind of manipulation, and they are confident that they can do this without anyone really noticing it at all.

Conclusion

Congratulations on making it through to the end of Manipulation: Highly Effective Persuasion and Manipulation Techniques People of Power Use for Deception and Influence, Including Seven Laws of Human Behavior, NLP Tips, and Strategies of Dark Psychology.

This book should have been informative and provided you with all the answers to your questions.

We hope it helped you to understand not just the ways through which people manipulate you but also powerful ways in which you can immunize yourself against manipulators.

The next step is to simply use all the powerful strategies and techniques used in the book to understand manipulative motives and to prevent people from manipulating you in relationships, at work, and within your social circle.

There are plenty of practical tips, wisdom nuggets, and real-life illustrations to help you gain a solid understanding of how manipulation works and how it can be fought in your everyday life.

Check out more books by Steven Turner

Printed in Great Britain
by Amazon